MW01146185

DO Drops

Volume 1

DO Drops

Volume 1

Daily Bible Devotional

Dr. Bo Wagner

Word of His Mouth Publishers
Mooresboro, NC

All Scripture quotations are taken from the **King James Version** of the Bible.

ISBN: 978-1-941039-40-3
Printed in the United States of America
©2019 Dr. Bo Wagner (Robert Arthur Wagner)

Word of His Mouth Publishers
Mooresboro, NC 28114
www.wordofhismouth.com

All rights reserved. No part of this publication may be reproduced in any form without the prior written permission of the publisher except for quotations in printed reviews.

Cover art by Chip Nuhrah

Devotion 1

Moses was dead, but the children of Israel still had the land of Canaan in front of them and needed to be led into it. For His part, God was not troubled by the death of Moses in regard to this task. He always has a man prepared for what lays ahead, and this was no exception.

Joshua 1:1 *Now a fter the death of Moses the servant of the LORD it came to pass, that the LORD spake unto Joshua the son of Nun, Moses' minister, saying,* **2** *Moses my servant is dead; now therefore arise, go over this Jordan, thou, and all this people, unto the land which I do give to them, even to the children of Israel.*

If "Moses is dead," had been all that was said, the children of Israel would have been in quite a predicament! But God spoke those words to Joshua and then gave him the task to lead the people into the Promised Land. Joshua had been through decades of training; God knew this moment was coming, and He had His man ready.

It is wonderful to have a godly leader to lean on. But the common denominator of our faith is not the leader but the God who provides one leader, then another, then another.

DO follow the godly leaders God gives you. But far more than that, DO have confidence that God still lives and leads even when those we are following grow old and die.

Personal Notes:

Devotion 2

As God began to give Joshua instructions on the taking of the land, He had some things to say to Joshua personally.

Joshua 1:6 *Be strong and of a good courage: for unto this people shalt thou divide for an inheritance the land, which I sware unto their fathers to give them.* **7** *Only be thou strong and very courageous, that thou mayest observe to do according to all the law, which Moses my servant commanded thee: turn not from it to the right hand or to the left, that thou mayest prosper whithersoever thou goest.*

Twice God commanded Joshua to be strong and of good courage. Two things are interesting about that. One, strength and courage were tied together. Two, since both were commands, then both were choices to be made! We would think that a person who is just naturally strong would therefore have courage on that basis. In other words, we would think that only courage is the choice and that it would be an easy choice.

But God placed both strength and courage into the category of choice. You see, it was not physical strength He was speaking of. No matter how strong Joshua could ever be in arms or chest or legs, Canaan was still too tough of a task. It would take God to knock down walls and cut giants down to size, therefore, the strength needed was spiritual not physical.

When we make the choice to be spiritually strong, the courage to fight physical and other kinds of battles will come easy.

DO choose to engage in all of the spiritual disciplines that make a believer strong in the Lord, and then DO go forth in courage and fight every battle God lays out ahead of you!

Personal Notes:

_____

_____

_____

_____

_____

_____

_____

_____

_____

_____

_____

_____

_____

_____

_____

_____

_____

_____

_____

_____

_____

_____

_____

_____

_____

Devotion 3

Before the children of Israel crossed over the Jordan, two and a half tribes had made request to stay on that eastern side since the land was good for their flocks and herds. This had caused quite the brouhaha, until they explained that they would still cross over Jordan and fight alongside all of the other tribes until the land was subdued. Then, and only then would they go and take possession of their own land.

Now Joshua was in command, and the time had come for Israel to go fight and for those two and one-half tribes to honor their vow. Joshua reminded them of that, and here is how they answered:

Joshua 1:16 *And they answered Joshua, saying, All that thou commandest us we will do, and whithersoever thou sendest us, we will go.* **17** *According as we hearkened unto Moses in all things, so will we hearken unto thee: only the LORD thy God be with thee, as he was with Moses.*

Do you ever wish you could see the facial expressions of the people in the Bible? Knowing what you know about how regularly the children of Israel disobeyed Moses and caused him fits, what must the look on Joshua's face have been like as he heard them say, "We will obey you just like we did Moses!"

If there was such a thing as a wilderness Walmart, I suspect his next stop would have been the aisle with the Tylenol and Maalox.

DO be so faithful and so dependable that, if you ever tell someone that you are going to be just as faithful and dependable as you always have been, they are encouraged by that statement, rather than terrified by it!

Personal Notes:

_____
_____
_____
_____
_____
_____
_____
_____
_____
_____
_____
_____
_____
_____
_____
_____
_____
_____
_____
_____
_____
_____
_____
_____
_____

Devotion 4

Forty years earlier, twelve spies had gone into the Promised Land. They had been sent in, not to see if they could take the land but to see the land they were going to take. But when they came back and delivered their report, it was a split report. Ten of them declared in no uncertain terms that the land could not be taken; there were giants there, and "we were like grasshoppers in their sight."

Two of them, though, declared with equal certainty that the land most certainly could be taken, and that those giants were "bread for us."

The two who gave the report of faith rather than the report of fear had names that we still know and remember: Joshua and Caleb.

Since the people followed the evil report, Israel was consigned to another thirty-eight years of wandering in the wilderness. But now, after all of these years, it was time to try again. And this time, in one of the most famous chapters of Scripture, things were radically different. Joshua 2 gives us the famous story of Rahab. But it also gives us the sequel to the saga of the spies. Look at the beginning and end of this sequel:

Joshua 2:1 *And Joshua the son of Nun sent out of Shittim two men to spy secretly, saying, Go view the land, even Jericho. And they went, and came into an harlot's house, named Rahab, and lodged there.*

Joshua 2:24 *And they said unto Joshua, Truly the LORD hath delivered into our hands all the land; for even all the inhabitants of the country do faint because of us.*

Where one generation failed, another succeeded. What one generation did became a warning to the next generation, not an anchor.

We are not, at all, ever bound to make the same foolish decisions as anyone who has ever come before us. We all get to choose what path we will take. The day that the past becomes an anchor rather than a guide, we need to cut the rope and let the anchor sink.

DO make up your mind to learn from the mistakes of the past, but never, ever be bound to them!

Personal Notes:

_____

_____

_____

_____

_____

_____

_____

_____

_____

_____

_____

_____

_____

_____

_____

_____

_____

_____

_____

_____

Devotion 5

The children of Israel were about to cross over the Jordan River and begin their conquest of the Promised Land. Before they did, though, God gave them a very specific instruction to follow:

Joshua 3:1 *And Joshua rose early in the morning; and they removed from Shittim, and came to Jordan, he and all the children of Israel, and lodged there before they passed over. 2 And it came to pass after three days, that the officers went through the host; 3 And they commanded the people, saying, When ye see the ark of the covenant of the LORD your God, and the priests the Levites bearing it, then ye shall remove from your place, and go after it. 4 Yet there shall be a space between you and it, about two thousand cubits by measure: come not near unto it, that ye may know the way by which ye must go: for ye have not passed this way heretofore.*

Notice that they were to follow the ark of God, but they were to do so from a distance of 2,000 cubits, meaning roughly 3,000 feet. Does it strike you as interesting that they would be required to follow, but to follow that far behind?

There is an important principle taught in this odd command. We are to follow God, but we are not to "crowd" God. Have you ever had the "joy" of having to endure a backseat driver, determined to tell the person behind the wheel where to turn, how fast to go, to look out for things in the other lane?

God does not like that kind of thing any more than we do!

DO follow God every day and every step of your life. But do not ever crowd Him; there is only one steering wheel, and the only hands that belong on it are His!

Personal Notes:

_____

_____

_____

_____

_____

_____

_____

_____

_____

_____

_____

_____

_____

_____

_____

_____

_____

_____

_____

_____

_____

_____

_____

_____

_____

Devotion 6

When one individual needs to cross a river, he can perhaps simply swim. But when an entire nation needs to cross a river, complete with all of the supplies that they are carrying, swimming is most definitely not an option.

It was time for the children of Israel to cross the Jordan, and something would need to be done to allow them to do so. And boy, was something ever done:

Joshua 3:14 *And it came to pass, when the people removed from their tents, to pass over Jordan, and the priests bearing the ark of the covenant before the people;* **15** *And as they that bare the ark were come unto Jordan, and the feet of the priests that bare the ark were dipped in the brim of the water, (for Jordan overfloweth all his banks all the time of harvest,)* **16** *That the waters which came down from above stood and rose up upon an heap very far from the city Adam, that is beside Zaretan: and those that came down toward the sea of the plain, even the salt sea, failed, and were cut off: and the people passed over right against Jericho.* **17** *And the priests that bare the ark of the covenant of the LORD stood firm on dry ground in the midst of Jordan, and all the Israelites passed over on dry ground, until all the people were passed clean over Jordan.*

As if a giant invisible dam had been put in place, the waters of the Jordan River stopped dead and stacked up. The people crossed over on dry ground, just as forty years ago their fathers and grandfathers had crossed over the dry ground of the Red Sea. The waters were different; one was a sea and one was a river, but the miracle was the same and the God of the miracle was the same.

When you face problems in your life that are not quite what you have faced before, DO remember that the "difference" of the problem is not the issue; the "sameness" of your God is the issue! If the God who dried up the Red Sea is the God who stopped the waters of the Jordan and the God who walked on water, then He is still the God that can handle whatever weird and unusual problem you may face.

Personal Notes:

_____

_____

_____

_____

_____

_____

_____

_____

_____

_____

_____

_____

_____

_____

_____

_____

_____

_____

_____

_____

Devotion 7

As the children of Israel prepared to go over the Jordan, God gave them a command that as they did, they were to take twelve large stones out of the riverbed and carry them over to the other side. The last few verses of the chapter tell us that they did so and explain to us the very important reason for the command.

Joshua 4:20 *And those twelve stones, which they took out of Jordan, did Joshua pitch in Gilgal.* **21** *And he spake unto the children of Israel, saying, When your children shall ask their fathers in time to come, saying, What mean these stones?* **22** *Then ye shall let your children know, saying, Israel came over this Jordan on dry land.* **23** *For the LORD your God dried up the waters of Jordan from before you, until ye were passed over, as the LORD your God did to the Red sea, which he dried up from before us, until we were gone over:* **24** *That all the people of the earth might know the hand of the LORD, that it is mighty: that ye might fear the LORD your God for ever.*

The stones that they took out of the river they set up on top of each other as a pillar. The specific reason for this is so that their children and future generations who had not seen the great miracle there at the river would ask about the pillar of stones, thus giving their parents a chance to tell them what had happened.

This principle of setting up "markers," visible reminders, of the goodness of God in our lives, is a good one. A child that sees those things and hears the stories of what God has done for his or her parents, will likely be a child anxious to see God do similar things in his or her own life.

DO set up tangible visible memory markers in your home and in your life, and then be prepared to tell your children what they mean!

Personal Notes:

_____

_____

_____

_____

_____

_____

_____

_____

_____

_____

_____

_____

_____

_____

_____

_____

_____

_____

_____

_____

_____

_____

_____

_____

Devotion 8

As the children of Israel wandered in the wilderness for forty years, they were miraculously sustained day by day with manna from heaven. The first few days and weeks, perhaps even the first few months, some of them would have been amazed at this heavenly provision.

But as the months and years dragged on, there would have been a greater and greater tendency to write it off as a coincidence, just a normal fact of life. But for anyone thinking that, they were about to get a reminder of how very miraculous it was:

Joshua 5:10 *And the children of Israel encamped in Gilgal, and kept the passover on the fourteenth day of the month at even in the plains of Jericho. 11 And they did eat of the old corn of the land on the morrow after the passover, unleavened cakes, and parched corn in the selfsame day. 12 And the manna ceased on the morrow after they had eaten of the old corn of the land; neither had the children of Israel manna any more; but they did eat of the fruit of the land of Canaan that year.*

Exactly one day after the children of Israel crossed over into the land and began to eat the produce in the fields of the land, the manna stopped. If it had continued, it could perhaps have been written off as a coincidence. But the fact that it lasted exactly as long as it needed to and then stopped when it was no longer needed, was another reminder that it was divinely appointed, and heaven sent.

DO learn that sometimes God reminds us of His goodness by what He gives, but sometimes He

even reminds us of His goodness by what He ceases
to give!

Personal Notes:

_____

_____

_____

_____

_____

_____

_____

_____

_____

_____

_____

_____

_____

_____

_____

_____

_____

_____

_____

_____

_____

_____

_____

_____

_____

_____

_____

Devotion 9

Joshua 6 is one of the most famous chapters in the Bible, containing the great account of the conquest of Jericho. Who could ever forget learning about the army that simply walked around the city one time a day for six days, and then seven times the seventh day, shouted, and saw the walls fall down flat before them?

But this chapter does not just tell us about God's army, Jericho's army, the walls, and the city. It also gives us the story of one seemingly insignificant person, Rahab the harlot. And for Rahab, this part of her story went very well indeed. After she received the spies and kept them safe, after she proclaimed her faith in the God of Israel, she was assured that her life and the life of her family would be spared. And that is exactly what happened.

Joshua 6:23 *And the young men that were spies went in, and brought out Rahab, and her father, and her mother, and her brethren, and all that she had; and they brought out all her kindred, and left them without the camp of Israel.* **24** *And they burnt the city with fire, and all that was therein: only the silver, and the gold, and the vessels of brass and of iron, they put into the treasury of the house of the LORD.* **25** *And Joshua saved Rahab the harlot alive, and her father's household, and all that she had; and she dwelleth in Israel even unto this day; because she hid the messengers, which Joshua sent to spy out Jericho.*

Do you find it amazing that the God of all power, the God able to make the walls of the city fall down flat at just over one word from His lips, would take time to care about someone so stained and insignificant as Rahab?

Every time the devil reminds you that you are nothing, DO remind him that your God just happens to love and care for "nothings!"

Personal Notes:

_____

_____

_____

_____

_____

_____

_____

_____

_____

_____

_____

_____

_____

_____

_____

_____

_____

_____

_____

_____

_____

_____

_____

_____

_____

_____

Devotion 10

In Joshua 7 Israel was fresh off their great victory against the mighty city of Jericho. The next place on the list of conquest was a tiny town called Ai. They went against that city, and, much to their surprise, things did not go well at all:

Joshua 7:5 *And the men of Ai smote of them about thirty and six men: for they chased them from before the gate even unto Shebarim, and smote them in the going down: wherefore the hearts of the people melted, and became as water.*

Thirty-six men, dead. Thirty-six graves for sons, fathers, husbands. Thirty-six reasons for the very harsh judgment of God that followed once they realized it was the sin of Achan that caused all of it:

Joshua 7:24 *And Joshua, and all Israel with him, took Achan the son of Zerah, and the silver, and the garment, and the wedge of gold, and his sons, and his daughters, and his oxen, and his asses, and his sheep, and his tent, and all that he had: and they brought them unto the valley of Achor.* **25** *And Joshua said, Why hast thou troubled us? the LORD shall trouble thee this day. And all Israel stoned him with stones, and burned them with fire, after they had stoned them with stones.*

The family of Achan would have had to be complicit in all of his theft in order for him to be able to hide everything he had stolen in the tent. It was his idea; but all of them paid the price.

Before you ever choose to do anything wrong, DO take stock of the fact that you may do wrong alone, but you are not likely to suffer all of the fallout alone. If you truly love those that you say you love, always do right!

Personal Notes:

_____
_____
_____
_____
_____
_____
_____
_____
_____
_____
_____
_____
_____
_____
_____
_____
_____
_____
_____
_____
_____
_____
_____
_____
_____
_____

Devotion 11

One of the failures in the attempted conquest of Ai was that no one ever asked God for His counsel on how to conduct the battle. Had they done so, He would most assuredly have made them aware of the sin in the camp and had them deal with that first.

They would not make that mistake again.

Joshua 8:1 *And the LORD said unto Joshua, Fear not, neither be thou dismayed: take all the people of war with thee, and arise, go up to Ai: see, I have given into thy hand the king of Ai, and his people, and his city, and his land: 2 And thou shalt do to Ai and her king as thou didst unto Jericho and her king: only the spoil thereof, and the cattle thereof, shall ye take for a prey unto yourselves: lay thee an ambush for the city behind it.*

In the first attempt at conquering Ai, they underestimated their opponent and only took a few thousand men. This time, hearing from the Lord first, they were told to take everyone.

There are two mistakes that people make on an all too regular basis: overestimating their own strength and underestimating the strength of an adversary.

DO realize that any of us are capable of losing any battle, physical or spiritual. That being the case, we should be wise and humble enough to seek God's guidance ahead of time and find out how He would have us conduct the battle.

Personal Notes:

_____
_____
_____
_____
_____
_____
_____
_____
_____
_____
_____
_____
_____
_____
_____
_____
_____
_____
_____
_____
_____
_____
_____
_____
_____
_____
_____
_____

Devotion 12

During the battle for Jericho, God had commanded that there would be no "spoils of war" for the people. Achan, in the midst of the battle, saw some gold and silver and a Babylonian garment and determined to take them for himself rather than obeying God's command. Thirty-six men then died in the next battle as a result of his sin, and he and his family were put to death.

But just hours later they went to battle against Ai again, and here is an interesting thing that we find:

Joshua 8:27 *Only the cattle and the spoil of that city Israel took for a prey unto themselves, according unto the word of the LORD which he commanded Joshua.*

Whereas God told them not to take the spoil from Jericho, He allowed them to take all the spoil from Ai. If Achan had simply been patient, he would have gotten every right thing his heart desired and then some.

And how often are we just like that? How often do we have to have what we want right now, rather than waiting for God's proper timing? Premarital sex, getting into debt for things we cannot afford, demanding a position for which we are not properly prepared, all of these and more are symptoms of the impatience that plagued Achan and still troubles all of us today.

DO be patient. God does not desire to withhold any good thing from us; He merely desires to make sure that we get all good things in the proper time.

Personal Notes:

_____

_____

_____

_____

_____

_____

_____

_____

_____

_____

_____

_____

_____

_____

_____

_____

_____

_____

_____

_____

_____

_____

_____

_____

_____

_____

_____

Devotion 13

While not much is ever said or preached about it, one of the most visually powerful scenes in all of Jewish history happened at the end of Joshua 8.

Joshua 8:33 *And all Israel, and their elders, and officers, and their judges, stood on this side the ark and on that side before the priests the Levites, which bare the ark of the covenant of the LORD, as well the stranger, as he that was born among them; half of them over against mount Gerizim, and half of them over against mount Ebal; as Moses the servant of the LORD had commanded before, that they should bless the people of Israel.* **34** *And afterward he read all the words of the law, the blessings and cursings, according to all that is written in the book of the law.* **35** *There was not a word of all that Moses commanded, which Joshua read not before all the congregation of Israel, with the women, and the little ones, and the strangers that were conversant among them.*

With half of the nation standing over against mount Gerizim and half of them standing over against mount Ebal, Joshua read all the words of the law, meaning most of the first five books of the Bible. Can you imagine the sound echoing off the hills as the written Word of God was read aloud to an entire nation!

In our day among some very popular, nationally known preachers, there is a strong tendency to minimize the importance of the written Word of God. But one place you will never find a tendency to minimize the importance of the written Word of God is within the written Word of God itself!

28

Even Jesus when tempted by the devil did not say, "Do you know who I am?" Instead, three times He said, "It is written…"

DO cherish your Bible. Read it every day, memorize it, trust it. If it was good for an entire nation, it is good for you and me and our families.

Personal Notes:

_____

_____

_____

_____

_____

_____

_____

_____

_____

_____

_____

_____

_____

_____

_____

_____

_____

_____

_____

_____

_____

Devotion 14

In Joshua 9 we are introduced to the "Gibeonite Traveling Stage Show," as it were.

Joshua 9:1 *And it came to pass, when all the kings which were on this side Jordan, in the hills, and in the valleys, and in all the coasts of the great sea over against Lebanon, the Hittite, and the Amorite, the Canaanite, the Perizzite, the Hivite, and the Jebusite, heard thereof;* **2** *That they gathered themselves together, to fight with Joshua and with Israel, with one accord.* **3** *And when the inhabitants of Gibeon heard what Joshua had done unto Jericho and to Ai,* **4** *They did work wilily, and went and made as if they had been ambassadors, and took old sacks upon their asses, and wine bottles, old, and rent, and bound up;* **5** *And old shoes and clouted upon their feet, and old garments upon them; and all the bread of their provision was dry and mouldy.* **6** *And they went to Joshua unto the camp at Gilgal, and said unto him, and to the men of Israel, We be come from a far country: now therefore make ye a league with us.*

God had commanded that no league be made with any of the inhabitants of the land. Knowing this, the Gibeonites put on an Oscar worthy performance, complete with costumes, props, and acting that would make Sir Laurence Olivier swell with pride.

But they were lying. Everything looked and seemed real, but they were lying.

DO be aware of the fact that throughout your life, people will put on epic performances and lie straight to your face. This is why, political correctness and social justice warriors notwithstanding, we should always wait for the evidence to come in before we make any decisions or decide who to believe!

Personal Notes:

_____

_____

_____

_____

_____

_____

_____

_____

_____

_____

_____

_____

_____

_____

_____

_____

_____

_____

_____

_____

_____

_____

_____

_____

_____

_____

_____

_____

Devotion 15

The Gibeonites pulled a fast one on Israel. But the real problem that allowed it to happen was that Israel made the exact same mistake they made before going to fight Ai; they did not ask God before they made their decision:

Joshua 9:14 *And the men took of their victuals, and asked not counsel at the mouth of the LORD.* **15** *And Joshua made peace with them, and made a league with them, to let them live: and the princes of the congregation sware unto them.* **16** *And it came to pass at the end of three days after they had made a league with them, that they heard that they were their neighbours, and that they dwelt among them.*

Behold Israel's second "uh oh" moment during the conquest of Canaan.

We live in a world that is deceptive and hard to figure out. That being the case, we need to be exceptionally prayerful and careful. Sometimes what seems to be such an obvious decision may not be nearly as obvious as we think, and a good time of prayer before the Lord may very well be what it takes to make that known to us.

DO pray before you say!

Personal Notes:

_____

_____

_____

_____

_____

_____

_____

_____

_____

_____

_____

_____

_____

_____

_____

_____

_____

_____

_____

_____

_____

_____

_____

_____

_____

_____

_____

_____

Devotion 16

There is no disputing that the Gibeonites lied, they did wrong. And yet, as we read their rationale, we find a kernel of good within it.

Joshua 9:22 *And Joshua called for them, and he spake unto them, saying, Wherefore have ye beguiled us, saying, We are very far from you; when ye dwell among us? 23 Now therefore ye are cursed, and there shall none of you be freed from being bondmen, and hewers of wood and drawers of water for the house of my God. 24 And they answered Joshua, and said, Because it was certainly told thy servants, how that the LORD thy God commanded his servant Moses to give you all the land, and to destroy all the inhabitants of the land from before you, therefore we were sore afraid of our lives because of you, and have done this thing. 25 And now, behold, we are in thine hand: as it seemeth good and right unto thee to do unto us, do. 26 And so did he unto them, and delivered them out of the hand of the children of Israel, that they slew them not. 27 And Joshua made them that day hewers of wood and drawers of water for the congregation, and for the altar of the LORD, even unto this day, in the place which he should choose.*

Did you catch the kernel of good that I spoke of? These people feared the Lord when the children of Israel themselves often did not!

How sad is it when the lost world has a healthier fear of God than many who call themselves believers? DO make sure that your fear of God is always healthy enough to exceed the fear of God of those who do not even know Him!

Personal Notes:

Devotion 17

In Joshua 10 the new "we didn't want them to begin with" allies of Israel, the Gibeonites, were attacked by their own countrymen. This resulted in Joshua and the army of Israel having to rush to their aid. They were winning the battle, but the sun was going down, and Joshua knew that many of the enemy would escape and regroup.

So, he prayed an unthinkably huge prayer:

Joshua 10:12 *Then spake Joshua to the LORD in the day when the LORD delivered up the Amorites before the children of Israel, and he said in the sight of Israel, Sun, stand thou still upon Gibeon; and thou, Moon, in the valley of Ajalon.* **13** *And the sun stood still, and the moon stayed, until the people had avenged themselves upon their enemies. Is not this written in the book of Jasher? So the sun stood still in the midst of heaven, and hasted not to go down about a whole day.* **14** *And there was no day like that before it or after it, that the LORD hearkened unto the voice of a man: for the LORD fought for Israel.*

The sun was on the verge of going down; the moon was already in the sky. And yet it just stopped... it stayed there about an extra day's worth of time, until they won the entire battle.

I cannot begin to wrap my mind around all of the scientific details that God accounted for in order to do that. I just know that Joshua had a good sense of how big God really is in order to pray a prayer that big!

It kind of makes you think that sometimes we pray as if our God is very small.

We have a very big God; so DO pray very big prayers!

Personal Notes:

_____

_____

_____

_____

_____

_____

_____

_____

_____

_____

_____

_____

_____

_____

_____

_____

_____

_____

_____

_____

_____

_____

_____

_____

_____

_____

_____

_____

_____

Devotion 18

The end of Joshua 10 and all of Joshua 11 is a recounting of all of the different battle campaigns Joshua and the children of Israel fought against the Canaanites. One verse in chapter eleven summarizes it for us this way:

Joshua 11:18 *Joshua made war a long time with all those kings.*

That verse is very interesting, don't you think? Canaan was their "Promised Land," and yet, in order to receive the promise, they had to battle for it year after year after year!

The best promises are almost always like that. God preserves His choicest treasures for those who are willing to faithfully serve Him and fight the spiritual battles that this world presents for as long a time as is necessary to win.

DO be long term in your outlook concerning the promises of God. The best of the best of those promises are liable to only come after years and years of struggle, but they will always be worth it.

Personal Notes:

_____
_____
_____
_____
_____
_____
_____
_____
_____
_____
_____
_____
_____
_____
_____
_____
_____
_____
_____
_____
_____
_____
_____
_____
_____
_____
_____
_____

Devotion 19

The twenty-four verses of Joshua 12 are what some people would consider "boring reading." It is simply a list of the names of the kings that Joshua and the children of Israel conquered in the Promised Land.

Here are a couple of verses to show you the kind of "riveting reading" we are talking about.

Joshua 12:9 *The king of Jericho, one; the king of Ai, which is beside Bethel, one;* **10** *The king of Jerusalem, one; the king of Hebron, one;* **11** *The king of Jarmuth, one; the king of Lachish, one;*

Why do we need to know this? Why take up space in Scripture for things that make our eyes cross rather than filling everything with miracles and great battles and adventure?

Here is your answer: because the historical, verifiable facts that are presented to us in Scripture let us know that the Bible is not a storybook but a history book! The kings and cities and nations mentioned were known to everyone in that era. If the Bible had simply been made up, it would never ever have come to be regarded as the Word of God, because everyone would be able to compare the "fiction" within it to the reality around them!

DO understand that the Bible, including all of the miracles, is the literal history of everything thatc happened, and all of the tiny details that we are tempted to snooze our way through as we read it serve as proof to its veracity.

Personal Notes:

_____

_____

_____

_____

_____

_____

_____

_____

_____

_____

_____

_____

_____

_____

_____

_____

_____

_____

_____

_____

_____

_____

_____

_____

_____

_____

Devotion 20

Joshua 11:15 tells us that Joshua obeyed all that the Lord had commanded him through Moses. And yet as we come to the first verse of chapter thirteen we read these words: **Joshua 13:1** *Now Joshua was old and stricken in years; and the Lord said unto him, Thou art old and stricken in years, and there remaineth yet very much land to be possessed.*

Joshua was old, he had spent his life being both energetic and obedient, and yet as his life came to a close there was still much work left to be done.

Do you ever feel that way? I do not really remember a time where I looked at the to do list and said, "Oh, look, there is nothing left to do!" Now do you see why it is so very important that we train new generations for Christ?

DO remember that the work that we are doing for the Lord will have to be passed down to our children and our grandchildren. If we have not diligently prepared them both in church and in our homes to follow in our footsteps as we serve the Lord, the baton will be dropped and the things that the Lord desires to accomplish through us will not be done. So, don't just serve the Lord, teach your children and grandchildren to do so as well!

Personal Notes:

_____
_____
_____
_____
_____
_____
_____
_____
_____
_____
_____
_____
_____
_____
_____
_____
_____
_____
_____
_____
_____
_____
_____
_____
_____
_____
_____
_____

Devotion 21

The man Balaam is one of the most interesting men in the Bible. Back in the book of Numbers an enemy king hired him to curse the children of Israel. Rather than cursing Israel, though, he uttered one of the most glorious words of prophecy in favor of Israel, and even gave a prophecy of their coming Messiah and of the star that would herald His birth.

And yet as we come to **Joshua 13:22** we read these words: *Balaam also the son of Beor, the soothsayer, did the children of Israel slay with the sword among them that were slain by them.*

Despite his great word of prophecy, Balaam continued to be a wicked man, a soothsayer, and Scripture tells us that he lured Israel to sin by parading Moabite women in front of them with whom they committed fornication. When the children of Israel went on to conquer the land, they had to put Balaam to death. His head knowledge was superb; he knew everything he needed to know about God. And yet that head knowledge never translated into a humbling of himself before that God.

DO remember that the facts you know about God are not what ultimately matters; whether or not you humble yourself before that God and serve and obey Him is what really matters.

Personal Notes:

_____
_____
_____
_____
_____
_____
_____
_____
_____
_____
_____
_____
_____
_____
_____
_____
_____
_____
_____
_____
_____
_____
_____
_____
_____
_____
_____
_____

Devotion 22

In Joshua 14, Caleb came to speak to Joshua. Caleb and Joshua had been the two spies out of the twelve who brought a good report when they spied out the land in the days of Moses. Because of that, God promised that Caleb and Joshua would still be alive to inherit the land. So as Caleb spoke to Joshua, he reminded him of that promise. And then he asked a request of Joshua that could easily be misunderstood if we do not study it and think it through: **Joshua 14:12** *Now therefore give me this mountain, whereof the Lord spake in that day; for thou heardest in that day how the Anakims were there, and that the cities were great and fenced: if so be the Lord will be with me, then I shall be able to drive them out, as the Lord said.*

When Caleb said, "Give me this mountain," we could almost immediately jump to a faulty conclusion that he wanted to be rewarded with a prime piece of property simply because he had obeyed. But if you read the rest of the verse, you will notice that he mentioned that the mountain contained huge enemies and cities that would be very hard to be taken. In other words, at eighty-five years old Caleb was not asking for easy street; he was asking to be allowed to fight the hardest battles available.

DO make up your mind not to lay down your sword and die too early. If you have breath in your body, you can still be a spiritual warrior for the Lord. If He intended for you to be done fighting as a soldier for Christ, He would already have called you home!

Personal Notes:

_____

_____

_____

_____

_____

_____

_____

_____

_____

_____

_____

_____

_____

_____

_____

_____

_____

_____

_____

_____

_____

_____

_____

_____

_____

_____

_____

_____

Devotion 23

In our last devotion, we saw that Caleb was asking for the hardest battles to fight. So clearly Caleb was not a shrinking violet afraid to wade into a fight; he was a warrior who was more than willing to do so. And yet as we arrive in **Joshua 15:16** we read these words: *And Caleb said, He that smiteth Kirjath-sepher, and taketh it, to him will I give Achsah my daughter to wife.*

If we did not know the character of Caleb, we might be tempted to assume that he was afraid to fight this battle and was trying to hire a warrior using his daughter as a paycheck! But the truth is the exact opposite. As we read the next few verses, we find that Caleb was a father who loved his daughters fiercely; if they asked for something and it was a right something, he found a way to give it to them. So, Caleb was not trying to pawn off his daughter to get something done; Caleb was actually thinking of his daughter when he said what he said. As a father, Caleb wanted to make sure that any man he gave his daughter to was going to be a warrior, not a wimp!

DO remember, dads, that you loved that girl first, and you have a responsibility to give her away one day to someone who will take just as good care of her as you have. And daughters, you be sure and seek both the Lord's will and your father's in any potential mate, for both of them have your best interest at heart.

Personal Notes:

_____

_____

_____

_____

_____

_____

_____

_____

_____

_____

_____

_____

_____

_____

_____

_____

_____

_____

_____

_____

_____

_____

_____

_____

_____

_____

_____

_____

Devotion 24

As Joshua was dividing the land to the children of Israel in chapter seventeen, a unique exchange took place between him and the children of Joseph. Joseph had received his lot as an inheritance, and the tribe was unhappy with the size of it. They were a very numerous people and felt like they should be given more land. So, in verse fourteen the tribe asked Joshua about that and said, *Why hast thou given me but one lot and one portion to inherit seeing I am a great people...* Now look at how Joshua answered them in verse fifteen: **Joshua 17:15** *And Joshua answered them, If thou be a great people, then get thee up to the wood country , and cut down for thyself there in the land of the Perizzites and of the giants, if mount Ephraim be too narrow for thee.* They said, "We are a great people." Joshua said, "If you are that great, go conquer more land!"

DO remember that real greatness is never a matter simply of claiming; it is a matter of doing! As the old saying goes, the proof is in the pudding. Or as one of my former employers said many years ago, "More do; less talk!"

Personal Notes:

_____

_____

_____

_____

_____

_____

_____

_____

_____

_____

_____

_____

_____

_____

_____

_____

_____

_____

_____

_____

_____

_____

_____

_____

_____

_____

Devotion 25

By the time of Joshua 21, the conquest of the land of Canaan was mostly complete. As we come to verses forty-four and forty-five, we read these words: **Joshua 21:44** *And the Lord gave them rest round about, according to all that he sware unto their fathers: and there stood not a man of all their enemies before them; the Lord delivered all their enemies into their hand.* **45** *There failed not ought of any good thing which the Lord had spoken unto the house of Israel; all came to pass.*

The Lord gave them rest. Nothing failed of all the good things He had spoken to them. And yet, having read the first twenty-one chapters, we know that those blessings and that rest only came through conflict. Had they not been willing to fight the battles they would never have been allowed to enjoy the blessings!

DO remember that the blessings of God almost always come through the process of the spiritual battles that we are called on to face. Paul told Timothy to behave himself as "a good soldier of Jesus Christ." The Christian life is not an easy thing, it is a thing filled with daily battles. But for those who are willing to endure the spiritual struggles, for those who are willing to do right in the face of opposition, the end results are always the same—rest and blessings!

Personal Notes:

Devotion 26

In the first two verses of Joshua 22, we read some of the rarest words in the Old Testament: **Joshua 22:1** *Then Joshua called the Reubenites, and the Gadites, and the half tribe of Manasseh,* **2** *And said unto them, Ye have kept all that Moses the servant of the Lord commanded you, and have obeyed my voice in all that I commanded you:*

Think back on the children of Israel during all the wilderness wanderings and you will realize how rare of a thing this was! The people were constantly disobeying Moses, God's man. And yet here Joshua was able to commend two and a half tribes for completely obeying Moses and completely obeying him. They demonstrated that humility of spirit and that willingness to come under authority that God so very highly prizes.

Were Moses and Joshua not men? Certainly they were men; they were just men. But they were also more than that, they were God's anointed authority over the people. In every context, military, family, church, nation, etc., there is always an order and a structure of authority. It does not mean that anyone is better than anyone else, but it is an indication that God is an orderly and a structured God. Anyone who is unwilling to submit himself or herself to the authority of someone that God has placed over them not only makes a very poor follower but will also always make an extremely poor leader.

Think about it; before Joshua ever got to lead, he had to submit himself under the leadership of Moses!

DO be willing to come under authority; even Jesus Himself demonstrated this. **Philippians 2:8** tells us that He *became obedient unto death, even the death of the cross.* It is because of that that the next two verses tell us that God the Father has highly exalted Him. With God, humility and obedience always comes before advancement.

Personal Notes:

_____

_____

_____

_____

_____

_____

_____

_____

_____

_____

_____

_____

_____

_____

_____

_____

_____

_____

_____

_____

_____

_____

_____

Devotion 27

Joshua 22:3 *Ye have not left your brethren these many days unto this day, but have kept the charge of the commandment of the Lord your God.*

This verse follows up on the two verses from yesterday. Joshua commended the two and one-half tribes for their obedience. What he specifically had in mind was the fact that they honored their promise to help the other nine and one-half tribes conquer the land before they went back across the Jordan River to the possession that they had already received. Joshua in this verse commended them for keeping their promise, he commended them for having that rarest of qualities that is also among the most valuable of qualities – loyalty. They did not leave their brethren; they fought alongside them until the job was done.

I would venture to say that as you think back through your life there have been many very talented people that have come and gone. But those talented people are not necessarily going to be the ones that you remember the most and value the most. The people that you remember the most and value the most are those who have been loyal. Those who can be counted on are always precious, even if they are poor, unskilled, and uneducated. Loyalty elevates people to lofty positions in our mind that can never be achieved any other way. And the reason that is such a good thing is because not everyone can be rich, not everyone can be skilled, not everyone can be well educated, but absolutely anyone can be loyal!

DO be able to be counted on; DO be loyal!

Personal Notes:

_____

_____

_____

_____

_____

_____

_____

_____

_____

_____

_____

_____

_____

_____

_____

_____

_____

_____

_____

_____

_____

_____

_____

_____

_____

_____

Devotion 28

After Joshua commended the two and one-half tribes for their loyalty and obedience, he gave them leave to go across the Jordan into the land of their possession. And then we read this in **Joshua 22:10** *And when they came unto the borders of Jordan, that are in the land of Canaan, the children of Reuben and the children of Gad and the half tribe of Manasseh built there an altar by Jordan, a great altar to see to.*

These two and one-half tribes built a massive altar right there by the Jordan River. That act nearly caused a devastating civil war in the nation. The rest of the chapter tells us that when the nine and one-half tribes on the western side of the river realized what the two and one-half tribes on the eastern side of the river had done, they immediately gathered for war. They were not going to have the two and one-half tribes going into idolatry and worshiping some false god on a false altar!

There was just one problem: that was not what the altar was for. They had jumped to a conclusion, and their conclusion was completely false. The two and one-half tribes on the eastern side of the river quickly explained why they had built the altar. They were worried that since the Jordan River now stood between them and the rest of the nation, future generations on that far side of the river would think that they were not actually part of the nation and would not let their children and grandchildren come across the river to worship the Lord. They built the altar as a testimony and a symbol to the fact that they, too, were Israelites, they, too, were worshipers of

Jehovah God. When the rest of the nation realized this, the war was averted.

But why did a war almost take place to begin with? One reason: people jumped to a conclusion. **Proverbs 18:13** *He that answereth a matter before he heareth it, it is folly and shame unto him.*

DO be very, very afraid of jumping to conclusions! People who jump to conclusions tend to fall on their face a lot and do damage to themselves and others along the way.

Personal Notes:

_____

_____

_____

_____

_____

_____

_____

_____

_____

_____

_____

_____

_____

_____

_____

_____

_____

_____

_____

_____

Devotion 29

Our devotional thought for the day comes from one of the most famous verses in all of Scripture. **Joshua 24:15** *And if it seem evil unto you to serve the Lord, choose you this day whom ye will serve; whether the gods which your fathers served that were on the other side of the flood, or the gods of the Amorites, in whose land ye dwell: but as for me and my house, we will serve the Lord.*

As Joshua spoke these words, he was old and not too far from death. We often read these words in the context of a man making a decision for his family, a decision that the entire family will follow the Lord. And all of that is certainly true. But there is another part of this verse that I think often gets overlooked. Joshua looked the entire nation in the eyes and pointed out that they, the nation, may or may not even continue to follow the Lord. He knew and he verbalized the fact that the nation may depart from the Lord and go after false gods. So what Joshua was saying, among other things, is that even if the entire nation turned their back on God, he would not go with them in that nor would his family. Even if he and his family had to do right alone, they were going to do right. What incredible dedication to that which is right!

Anyone can do right in a crowd of others doing right; it takes character to do right going against the crowd. DO right at all times, even if it means doing right alone!

Personal Notes:

_____
_____
_____
_____
_____
_____
_____
_____
_____
_____
_____
_____
_____
_____
_____
_____
_____
_____
_____
_____
_____
_____
_____
_____
_____

Devotion 30

As Joshua was closing out his words to the children of Israel, he made an incredibly unique statement to them: **Joshua 24:27** *And Joshua said unto all the people, Behold, this stone shall be a witness unto us; for it hath heard all the words of the Lord which he spake unto us: it shall be therefore a witness unto you, lest ye deny your God.*

Joshua set a large stone in place by the sanctuary, and he spoke the words of the covenant to the children of Israel right there in that place. He then told them that the stone had heard all of the words of the Lord and would therefore be a witness against them if they disobeyed! There is absolutely no reason to take this figuratively; if God is God enough to make a rock and the entire universe out of nothing, then He is God enough to give rocks the ability to hear and to remember.

I wonder, therefore, how many times people have spoken words in secret with no one around, not even realizing that the rocks and the trees and the very wind of the air can hear what they are saying? **Matthew 12:36** *But I say unto you, That every idle word that men shall speak, they shall give account thereof in the day of judgment.*

DO remember that when you get right down to it, there is no such thing as a secret. So always do right!

Personal Notes:

_____
_____
_____
_____
_____
_____
_____
_____
_____
_____
_____
_____
_____
_____
_____
_____
_____
_____
_____
_____
_____
_____
_____
_____
_____
_____
_____
_____

Devotion 31

Joshua 24:32 is one of my very favorite verses: *And the bones of Joseph, which the children of Israel brought up out of Egypt, buried they in Shechem, in a parcel of ground which Jacob bought of the sons of Hamor the father of Shechem for an hundred pieces of silver: and it became the inheritance of the children of Joseph.* Joseph died four hundred years or so before this point. Before he died, he commanded that they not leave his bones in Egypt. He wanted his bones to be carried back to the Promised Land to be buried. Hundreds of years later, Moses led the children of Israel out of Egypt. And when he did, in addition to everything that everyone was carrying, someone was carrying a bag of bones! I often wonder what it was like to be the bag of bones carrier.

And yet, this odd and seemingly insignificant task was, in reality, so significant that it was recorded in Scripture for all future generations to see.

DO remember that there are no insignificant tasks in the service of the Lord!

Personal Notes:

_____
_____
_____
_____
_____
_____
_____
_____
_____
_____
_____
_____
_____
_____
_____
_____
_____
_____
_____
_____
_____
_____
_____
_____
_____

Devotion 32

The book of Judges marks a transitional time in the history of Israel when they moved from great leadership under Moses and Joshua to the eventual monarchy under Saul and David and the remaining kings. During this four hundred plus year period of time, it was constant warfare and battle in the Promised Land.

At the very beginning of the book of Judges, there was still much land left to be conquered, and Joshua was dead. So, the people, without Joshua, began the process of attempting to conquer the rest of their inheritance.

Judges 1:3 *And Judah said unto Simeon his brother, Come up with me into my lot, that we may fight against the Canaanites; and I likewise will go with thee into thy lot. So Simeon went with him.*

The nation of Israel, at this time, was much like the American colonies before the adoption of the Constitution. They were twelve individual tribes, in a loose confederation as a nation.

In the verse we just read, Judah was going to go to war for his part of the Promised Land. Before he did so, though, he contacted the tribe of Simeon and asked Simeon to come with him to the fight, promising to return the favor.

There is something of great spiritual value to learn here. We are always stronger when we fight our battles together! We face huge enemies; the world, the flesh, the devil. If God's people are in the habit of working together and supporting one another and praying for each other fervently, if we are as concerned for the welfare of our brothers and sisters in Christ as we are for our own welfare, we will be much better off.

DO fight your battles together, children of God; DO support one another

Personal Notes:

_____

_____

_____

_____

_____

_____

_____

_____

_____

_____

_____

_____

_____

_____

_____

_____

_____

_____

_____

_____

_____

_____

_____

_____

_____

Devotion 33

As Judah was battling for their portion of the Promised Land, they went to war against a king named Adoni-bezek. They captured this heathen king, and when they did, the Bible tells us this: **Judges 1:6** *But Adoni-bezek fled; and they pursued after him, and caught him, and cut off his thumbs and his great toes. 7 And Adoni-bezek said, Threescore and ten kings, having their thumbs and their great toes cut off, gathered their meat under my table: as I have done, so God hath requited me. And they brought him to Jerusalem, and there he died.*

A person without their thumbs and big toes is helpless, totally dependent upon others. It was a common practice when a nation captured an enemy king to treat them in this way. Adoni-bezek made it very clear that he himself was familiar with this; he had done it to seventy others before him. Now he was reaping what he had so often sown.

DO remember that the law of sowing and reaping is a law for the ages. In the ancient world, in the modern world, in any future world, the law of sowing and reaping will always apply, so be careful what you sow! As I say so often, "The choices you make plus the consequences that follow equal your life. Therefore, better decisions equal better results!"

Personal Notes:

_____
_____
_____
_____
_____
_____
_____
_____
_____
_____
_____
_____
_____
_____
_____
_____
_____
_____
_____
_____
_____
_____
_____
_____
_____

Devotion 34

Judges 1:19 *And the Lord was with Judah; and he drave out the inhabitants of the mountain; but could not drive out the inhabitants of the valley, because they had chariots of iron.*

This verse seems to present us with a spiritual conundrum. It tells us that the Lord was with Judah, and because of this, Judah won the victory over those who lived in the mountain. But the next thing it says is that Judah could not drive out the inhabitants of the valley because they had superior technology, namely chariots of iron. Is the Lord not great enough to handle chariots of iron? What in the world is this about? The answer begins to come in verse 28: **Judges 1:28** *And it came to pass, when Israel was strong, that they put the Canaanites to tribute, and did not utterly drive them out.* Notice that the "could not" of verse nineteen has turned into "did not" in verse twenty-eight. The power of God was enough to drive out the inhabitants of the mountain immediately. But God is not going to give us every victory immediately and easily.

Some victories He is going to expect us to struggle and work for, for our own benefit. The children of Israel eventually got strong enough in the power of God to drive out the all of the Canaanites, even with their chariots of iron. But by that time, they decided that it would be much more "advantageous" for them to keep them around as tributaries, taxpayers, rather than driving them out. In other words, by the time they were strong enough to do the job, they were spiritually weak enough to decide not to do the job. And because of that, the "could not" which became a "did not" in Judges 2:3 turned into a "will not".

That "will not" came from God: **Judges 2:3** *Wherefore I also said, I **will not** drive them out from before you; but they shall be as thorns in your sides, and their gods shall be a snare unto you.*

In other words, the spiritual ability they had to gain the victory was taken away from them.

DO realize two things. One, sometimes God will make us work very hard and for a very long time for spiritual victory. Two, if after we have gained the strength for that victory we back away from it and refuse to take it, God will remove the strength that He gave us to achieve that victory. So, go all out all the time all for God; the spiritual life is either victory or defeat, there really is no middle ground!

Personal Notes:

_____

_____

_____

_____

_____

_____

_____

_____

_____

_____

_____

_____

_____

_____

Devotion 35

Joshua was dead, and the future was uncertain for the children of Israel. It became much more uncertain and even much more grim with what we read in these verses: **Judges 2:10** *And also all that generation were gathered unto their fathers: and there arose another generation after them, which knew not the Lord , nor yet the works which he had done for Israel.* **11** *And the children of Israel did evil in the sight of the Lord , and served Baalim:*

There is a two-fold fault found in these verses. The first fault belongs to the older generation who somehow failed to pass on the baton of belief to the younger generation. They took time to fight the battles, but they did not seem to take enough time to draw their children into a walk with the God that they themselves had served. The second fault, though, was with the younger generation themselves. Each generation has a responsibility to seek after the God of their fathers. No young person should ever take it for granted that God will simply "pour Himself out all over them" with no effort on their behalf.

To the young people of this country, I have a warning message: seek God on your own, each and every day of your life. DO remember that each of us have a responsibility to pray until we see our own prayers answered, and to study God's word until we understand it for ourselves, and to worship God until we have a vibrant relationship with Him not dependent on anyone who has come before us!

Personal Notes:

_____
_____
_____
_____
_____
_____
_____
_____
_____
_____
_____
_____
_____
_____
_____
_____
_____
_____
_____
_____
_____
_____
_____
_____
_____
_____
_____

Devotion 36

The book of Judges was a constant repetitive cycle of the children of Israel disobeying, going into captivity, crying out to God, being sent a deliverer, being brought out of bondage, and then going back into sin to start the whole process all over again. The end of Judges 2:19 informs us of the root cause of all of the struggle: **Judges 2:19b** *...they ceased not from their own doings, nor from their stubborn way.*

Every bit of this was about stubbornness and rebellion; every bit of this was caused by the refusal to humble themselves before God, submit to Him, and obey Him.

In the spiritual life it is either going to be our will or God's will. And if we choose our own will, we will be choosing a constant cycle of disaster. If we choose His will, we will live in victory; it really is that simple.

DO remember that God's will must be supreme, and our will must be submitted. One thing God has never approved of for even a moment is a rebellious, stubborn heart.

Personal Notes:

_____
_____
_____
_____
_____
_____
_____
_____
_____
_____
_____
_____
_____
_____
_____
_____
_____
_____
_____
_____
_____
_____
_____
_____
_____
_____

Devotion 37

There was much, very much, that God had to say about Israel and their sin and stubbornness in the book of Judges. As we arrive in chapter three, He lists one that to Him was exceptionally grievous: **Judges 3:6** *And they took their daughters to be their wives, and gave their daughters to their sons, and served their gods.*

The children of Israel, God's covenant people, allowed and even encouraged their children to marry the lost young people around them.

There has never been and will never be, ever, a time when this is acceptable in His sight: **2 Corinthians 6:14** *Be ye not unequally yoked together with unbelievers: for what fellowship hath righteousness with unrighteousness? and what communion hath light with darkness?*

DO understand that God commands this for our own benefit. Each and every time the Israelites disobeyed, it did not result in the ungodly becoming godly; it resulted in the godly becoming ungodly. Love God more; love Him enough to keep yourself only for a saved mate and to demand the same of your children

Personal Notes:

_____
_____
_____
_____
_____
_____
_____
_____
_____
_____
_____
_____
_____
_____
_____
_____
_____
_____
_____
_____
_____
_____
_____
_____
_____

Devotion 38

The man Othniel is generally regarded as the first or one of the first judges of Israel. Here is what we read about him: **Judges 3:9** *And when the children of Israel cried unto the Lord, the Lord raised up a deliverer to the children of Israel, who delivered them, even Othniel the son of Kenaz, Caleb's younger brother.*

If you have been paying attention, the name Othniel should be a bit familiar to you: **Judges 1:12** *And Caleb said, He that smiteth Kirjath-sepher, and taketh it, to him will I give Achsah my daughter to wife.* **13** *And Othniel the son of Kenaz, Caleb's younger brother, took it: and he gave him Achsah his daughter to wife.*

In a previous devotion about this event, I pointed out that Caleb was more than capable of handling this fight on his own. He did what he did here to ensure that his daughter ended up married to a brave and courageous man, a man willing and able to fight when necessary. Now fast forward to the time and the fact that Othniel became a judge of Israel. This man fought a battle and won, a single battle. What he could not possibly have known was that that battle and that victory was in preparation for much greater things in his life.

Very often we wonder why we have to face the things we face and fight the battles we fight. But those things that we face and those battles we fight are often in preparation for much greater things that God has in store for our lives! God does not usually thrust the untested and unprepared into great service for Him. He uses those who have submitted to the

78

forging fires of testing and trials to do His greatest works.

DO remember, each and every day that you face trials and hardships, you are thinking very likely only of today, but God is thinking way down the line about all of the things that He has in store for you and all of the ways that He intends to use you when you come through these fires!

Personal Notes:

_____

_____

_____

_____

_____

_____

_____

_____

_____

_____

_____

_____

_____

_____

_____

_____

_____

_____

_____

_____

_____

_____

_____

Devotion 39

One of the judges of Israel was incredibly distinct from all of the others: **Judges 4:4** *And Deborah, a prophetess, the wife of Lapidoth, she judged Israel at that time.*

All through the book of Judges we are used to reading about men; strong, warlike, powerful men. And yet in this text it was not a man who led the nation, it was a woman. Deborah, appointed by God Himself, used as both a judge and a prophetess, not only lead the nation of Israel, she led them well. She ended up catapulting them to one of their greatest victories.

So often you will be told by the Bible-hating world how God and the Bible are anti-woman simply because God reserves the role of New Testament preacher for men. But nothing could be farther from the truth! Deborah is only one of a great many examples in Scripture of strong, powerful women that God used mightily.

Girls, DO realize that God intends to use you mightily. Whether He uses you as a mother or a worker or the President of the United States or something in between, God wants to use women as well as men to do great things.

Boys DO understand that God made both men and women, and He intends greatness for both!

Personal Notes:

_____

_____

_____

_____

_____

_____

_____

_____

_____

_____

_____

_____

_____

_____

_____

_____

_____

_____

_____

_____

_____

_____

_____

_____

_____

_____

_____

Devotion 40

In yesterday's devotion we looked at the great prophetess of Israel, Deborah the judge. But she is not the only great woman mentioned in Judges chapter 4.

Judges 4:21 *Then Jael Heber's wife took a nail of the tent, and took an hammer in her hand, and went softly unto him, and smote the nail into his temples, and fastened it into the ground: for he was fast asleep and weary. So he died.*

This woman, Jael, is one of the most fascinating characters in the Bible. Sisera, the enemy general, when the battle went against them as he was fighting against Israel, ran into her tent to hide. The people of her husband had some sort of a peace treaty between themselves and between the enemy king for whom Sisera worked.

In other words, this woman had a choice to make. Would she honor the treaty that was allowing Israel to be overrun, or would she utilize the opportunity that God had placed in her hands to free Israel? In order to take option number two, it was going to require her to step very far outside of what would be considered a "normal comfort zone." And she did. She took the tent spike and a hammer and drove the spike into his head all the way to the ground. Ouch...

DO understand that God is not particularly interested in us finding a "comfort zone" and hanging out there for our entire lives. All of us would love to do so. We would all love for life to be smooth and peaceful and comfortable with no ripples, no worries, no troubles, no struggles. But absolutely nothing great ever happens that way! Greatness, and especially greatness for God, only comes as we step out of our comfort zone and determine to do a work for Him no matter what!

Personal Notes:

_____

_____

_____

_____

_____

_____

_____

_____

_____

_____

_____

_____

_____

_____

_____

_____

_____

_____

_____

_____

_____

_____

_____

_____

_____

_____

Devotion 41

After the great battle that Deborah and the people of Israel won, thanks to a little lady with a tent spike and a hammer, Deborah and Barak began to sing. Yes, I know that sounds like a musical; "huge fight followed by impromptu singing and perfectly choreographed dancing…" But this was actually fairly common to Israel. After God gave them a great victory by dropping the Red Sea onto the armies of Egypt, they did the exact same thing.

But it is a phrase that they sang twice that is very interesting and very instructive: **Judges 5:2** *Praise ye the Lord for the avenging of Israel, when the people willingly offered themselves.* **Judges 5:9** *My heart is toward the governors of Israel, that offered themselves willingly among the people. Bless ye the Lord.*

Twice we read that the people "willingly offered themselves." We are reading about this battle and this victory in the past tense. For them, when they fought it, it was not the past tense. It was a present tense battle that they did not know whether they would win or lose. In fact, based on the information at hand, they would have been expected to lose. And yet they willingly offered themselves to fight a battle that logically they did not seem to have the ability to win. They willingly offered themselves. This is the exact same thing that God expects of us even today!

We may face overwhelming odds and situations that it does not seem like we can win. God is not looking to see if we can come up with good enough ideas or excellent enough strategies to win;

He just wants to see if we are willing to offer ourselves whether we win or whether we lose.

DO willingly offer yourself to the Lord for His service every single day. That is the first step toward victory, since it is God that gives the victory anyway!

Personal Notes:

_____
_____
_____
_____
_____
_____
_____
_____
_____
_____
_____
_____
_____
_____
_____
_____
_____
_____
_____
_____
_____
_____
_____
_____
_____
_____

Devotion 42

As Deborah and Barak continued to sing about the battle they had fought and the victory they had won, they came to a point in the song that lets us know that out of the twelve tribes of Israel, some came to the fight and some did not:

Judges 5:16 *Why abodest thou among the sheepfolds, to hear the bleatings of the flocks? For the divisions of Reuben there were great searchings of heart.* **17** *Gilead abode beyond Jordan: and why did Dan remain in ships? Asher continued on the sea shore, and abode in his breaches.* **18** *Zebulun and Naphtali were a people that jeoparded their lives unto the death in the high places of the field.*

There was a battle to be fought, but Reuben stayed at the sheepfolds. There was a battle to be fought, but Gilead (descended from Manasseh) stayed on the other side of Jordan. There was a battle to be fought, but Dan stayed with his ships, and Asher stayed there by the seashore. Zebulun and Naphtali are mentioned as two that came to the battle and risked their lives for themselves and others.

Israel did win the battle. Everyone, those who fought and those who did not fight, were able to enjoy the freedom that came from the victory. But how they went down in song was radically different.

When the song of our battles here and now are sung in heaven, what will be said of you? Did you quietly stay out of things and let others fight the battle, or did you strap on your spiritual armor and behave as a good soldier of Jesus Christ?

DO make sure that when the singing takes place in heaven as we gather on the street of gold, your name is listed in with those who fought rather than those who feared, those who labored rather than those who were lazy, and those who made a difference rather than those who did not make a dent!

Personal Notes:

_____

_____

_____

_____

_____

_____

_____

_____

_____

_____

_____

_____

_____

_____

_____

_____

_____

_____

_____

_____

_____

_____

_____

_____

_____

Devotion 43

As Deborah and Barak wrapped up their singing in Judges 5, there is a part of the song that seems to be a prophecy, a word from the Lord given to Deborah:

Judges 5:28 *The mother of Sisera looked out at a window, and cried through the lattice, Why is his chariot so long in coming? why tarry the wheels of his chariots?* **29** *Her wise ladies answered her, yea, she returned answer to herself,* **30** *Have they not sped? have they not divided the prey; to every man a damsel or two; to Sisera a prey of divers colours, a prey of divers colours of needlework, of divers colours of needlework on both sides, meet for the necks of them that take the spoil?*

There was an assumption on the part of Sisera's mother that just as he had always succeeded and gotten by with fighting against God's people, he surely had done so again. But what she did not know was that her son's time was up, and that God had put a stop to his wickedness.

We often wonder how long the wicked world will get by with hurting God's people. The answer is, "Not forever." There is an expiration date on all wickedness and on all wicked people; there is a point at which God says, "No more."

DO understand that wickedness and wicked people are temporary, but God and God's people and the ultimate victory He will give us are eternal!

Personal Notes:

_____
_____
_____
_____
_____
_____
_____
_____
_____
_____
_____
_____
_____
_____
_____
_____
_____
_____
_____
_____
_____
_____
_____
_____
_____
_____
_____
_____
_____
_____
_____
_____

Devotion 44

Judges 6 introduces us to Gideon, one of Israel's greatest judges. But there are two verses in this chapter that, when compared side by side, paint a bleak spiritual picture:

Judges 6:1 *And the children of Israel did evil in the sight of the Lord: and the Lord delivered them into the hand of Midian seven years.*

Judges 6:6 *And Israel was greatly impoverished because of the Midianites; and the children of Israel cried unto the Lord.*

Verse one that tells us that the children of Israel did evil in the sight of the Lord. The next several verses show them, because of that, falling under the domination of Midian. It is then that verse six tells us that Israel became greatly impoverished because of the Midianites, and at that point they "cried unto the Lord."

In other words, the fact that they were living in sin did not bother them enough to cry out for God's help, but when their financial situation began to be affected, that bothered them enough to cry out to God for help. How sad is it that the latter bothered them, but not the former!

DO regularly evaluate your own life to make sure that the things that ought to bother you actually bother you! As a child of God, nothing should bother us more than living in sin and not being right with God.

Personal Notes:

_____

_____

_____

_____

_____

_____

_____

_____

_____

_____

_____

_____

_____

_____

_____

_____

_____

_____

_____

_____

_____

_____

_____

_____

_____

_____

_____

Devotion 45

The introduction that Scripture gives us to the man Gideon is both historically accurate and incredibly funny:

Judges 6:11 *And there came an angel of the Lord , and sat under an oak which was in Ophrah, that pertained unto Joash the Abi-ezrite: and his son Gideon threshed wheat by the winepress, to hide it from the Midianites.* **12** *And the angel of the Lord appeared unto him, and said unto him, The Lord is with thee, thou mighty man of valour.*

An angel was sent from God to a man who was hiding in fear, and the first words he spoke to that man were "the Lord is with thee, thou mighty man of valor." Mighty man of valor? If there is anyone who did not see himself that way, it was Gideon! He rightfully saw himself as scared and insignificant. But God always sees the potential that He has built into a person, not just how they currently are at that moment…

People often say that if someone just believed in them, they could be great. Child of God, God does believe in you! He believes that you can be great for Him, not because you are great, but because in the words of **1 John 4:4** *Greater is he that is in you than he that is in the world!*

DO wake up every day with the realization that God sees you for all that you can be in His power. Now submit yourselves to Him, and go forth in that power, and be all that He knows you can be!

Personal Notes:

Devotion 46

As Gideon began the process of taking up the mantle as the next judge of Israel, he listened carefully to the instructions that God gave him as to how to begin. And one of the first instructions that God gave Gideon was, in some ways, disappointing:

Judges 6:25 *And it came to pass the same night, that the Lord said unto him, Take thy father's young bullock, even the second bullock of seven years old, and throw down the altar of Baal that thy father hath, and cut down the grove that is by it:*

Gideon's own father had built an altar to Baal... What in the world kind of a chance does a child have to turn out right when they grow up under that poor of a spiritual example! Yes, Gideon did go on to be right with God and to do a great work for God. But in order to do that, he had to throw down his own father's idolatrous altar.

Moms and dads, grandparents, will our children or grandchildren have to throw down some of our wicked altars in order to live right? It is always a sad state of affairs when children have to live right in spite of their parents or in spite of their grandparents rather than being able to walk in the godly footsteps of their parents and grandparents!

DO evaluate your own lives, adults, and make sure that you do not have any wicked altars standing that those who are coming after you will have to throw down in order to live for God!

Personal Notes:

_____
_____
_____
_____
_____
_____
_____
_____
_____
_____
_____
_____
_____
_____
_____
_____
_____
_____
_____
_____
_____
_____
_____
_____
_____
_____
_____

Devotion 47

We are still observing the life of Gideon as we arrive in Judges 7. In this chapter, God begins to speak to Gideon about the coming battle. He intends to give Israel victory over the Midianites. But something that He says in verse two is interesting on several levels:

Judges 7:2 *And the Lord said unto Gideon, The people that are with thee are too many for me to give the Midianites into their hands, lest Israel vaunt themselves against me, saying, Mine own hand hath saved me.*

It is, of course, interesting to note that while going toward a military campaign, God was insistent that they do so with less soldiers rather than more. I do not know many generals that would view things the same way! But what is much more interesting is the reason behind that. God told Gideon that if He allowed them to win the battle with all of the soldiers they had brought, that they would "vaunt themselves against him…" In other words, even if they won the victory in God's power, which was the only way they could have won it, if they had enough men to even remotely allow themselves to entertain the idea that they had done it, not only would they take credit for it, they would actually set themselves against God. They would brag about their power and become an enemy of the One who had actually given them the victory!

DO remember that humility makes us the ally of God, but pride always, every single time, makes us the enemy of God!

Personal Notes:

_____

_____

_____

_____

_____

_____

_____

_____

_____

_____

_____

_____

_____

_____

_____

_____

_____

_____

_____

_____

_____

_____

_____

_____

_____

_____

_____

Devotion 48

Before Gideon and Israel went to battle against the Midianites, God, knowing Gideon's fear, sent him down to the camp of the Midianites to overhear one of their conversations. He did this to give Gideon the extra courage he needed to lead and to fight the battle. What he heard when he got there was very unusual:

Judges 7:13 *And when Gideon was come, behold, there was a man that told a dream unto his fellow, and said, Behold, I dreamed a dream, and, lo, a cake of barley bread tumbled into the host of Midian, and came unto a tent, and smote it that it fell, and overturned it, that the tent lay along.*

The verses that follow let us know that the Midianites interpretation of the dream was that the loaf of barley bread represented Gideon himself. Barley bread, in our day, is expensive and sought after. But in Gideon's day the exact opposite was true; it was course, unrefined, dirt cheap bread that was usually only fed to animals. Gideon was being compared to a common, unwanted, inexpensive loaf of bread. And yet he was also being told that God was going to use him to accomplish one of the greatest victories of all times!

Do you ever feel common and cheap and worthless? DO rejoice every time you feel that way knowing that God is able to take the most common of things and do the most uncommon of tasks!

Personal Notes:

_____
_____
_____
_____
_____
_____
_____
_____
_____
_____
_____
_____
_____
_____
_____
_____
_____
_____
_____
_____
_____
_____
_____
_____
_____
_____
_____
_____

Devotion 49

The battle plan that God gave to Gideon to defeat the Midianites was incredibly unusual. In fact, it was well nigh unexplainable. Because of that, look what Gideon said to the people:

Judges 7:17 *And he said unto them, Look on me, and do likewise: and, behold, when I come to the outside of the camp, it shall be that, as I do, so shall ye do.*

"Just do what you see me do." That was the instructions that Gideon gave his followers! And the result was a resounding victory for which God was able to claim all glory.

But I wonder, how often can we safely say the same words that Gideon said? Gideon knew that he was in the center of God's will, living right, and that if people just did what they saw him do, they would be perfectly successful. Do we live so right, so much in the center of God's will, that we could just tell others to do as we do and have them become successful for God as well?

DO remember that one good example is worth 10,000 good words!

Personal Notes:

_____
_____
_____
_____
_____
_____
_____
_____
_____
_____
_____
_____
_____
_____
_____
_____
_____
_____
_____
_____
_____
_____
_____
_____
_____
_____
_____
_____

Devotion 50

After Gideon won the initial battle against the Midianites, the task turned to pursuing their fleeing enemies and destroying them before they could re-gather themselves and come against them again.

Judges 8:4 *And Gideon came to Jordan, and passed over, he, and the three hundred men that were with him, faint, yet pursuing them.*

Faint, yet pursuing. That has always struck me as one of the most profound phrases in Scripture. Gideon and his men were tired, exhausted, worn out... Have you ever been there? Do you sometimes or even often feel like you cannot put one foot in front of another? It gets like that in matters of spirituality, in the family, at the job, exhaustion becomes a part of life. And yet, the great success that Gideon experienced was as a direct result of the fact that he kept on going even when he felt like quitting.

Sometimes victory is just a matter of taking another step and then another step and then another step and then another step until we have won. DO make up your mind to continue to put one foot in front of the other, to continue to serve God, to continue to be faithful to your family, to continue to be an excellent employee or businessperson; just keep going. There are many substitutes for talent, but there is absolutely no substitute for persistence!

Personal Notes:

_____

_____

_____

_____

_____

_____

_____

_____

_____

_____

_____

_____

_____

_____

_____

_____

_____

_____

_____

_____

_____

_____

_____

_____

_____

_____

Devotion 51

While Gideon was pursuing his fleeing enemies, his men were tired and exhausted. They came to the city of Succoth, and Gideon asked for some loaves of bread for his men so that they would have the energy to continue the pursuit against everyone's common enemies. But the princes of Succoth had something very sarcastic to say in response to that request:

Judges 8:6 *And the princes of Succoth said, Are the hands of Zebah and Zalmunna now in thine hand, that we should give bread unto thine army?*

In other words, "It doesn't look to us like you have caught them yet; why should we risk our necks to help you when you might just lose?" These men were unwilling to risk anything for the side of righteousness unless they were one hundred percent certain that there was going to be a victory. In other words, they really were not willing to risk anything at all! They were cowards.

I cannot think of anything more despicable to be than a spiritual coward! There is a great spiritual battle raging for the souls of men across this world. We have been told to be good soldiers of Jesus Christ. Let us never be found among the ranks of the cowards who stick our fingers into the air to see which way the wind is blowing before we risk ourselves or our time or our resources to do something for God!

DO be brave, a pursuer of righteousness rather than a mere calculator of risk!

Personal Notes:

_____

_____

_____

_____

_____

_____

_____

_____

_____

_____

_____

_____

_____

_____

_____

_____

_____

_____

_____

_____

_____

_____

_____

_____

_____

_____

_____

_____

_____

Devotion 52

When Gideon returned from his successful pursuit of the kings of Midian and their hosts, he went back to the city of Succoth where the elders and princes of the city had, just one day earlier, sarcastically sent him on his way without any help or any bread for his weary men. Once he arrived, "school" was immediately in session:

Judges 8:16 *And he took the elders of the city, and thorns of the wilderness and briers, and with them he taught the men of Succoth.*

Gideon "taught" these elders and princes a lesson by spanking their hind ends with thorns and briars! For the record, there was a much easier way available for them to have learned. Had they simply studied their own history and the God who had so often given them victory over forces much greater than themselves, they would have known to give Gideon and his men the bread and resources they needed, they would have known to trust God for the victory to begin with.

But since they did not study their own history and since they did not study how God had so often worked in their lives, the only option left was for them to be taught in the most painful of manners!

DO be very easy to teach; DO be a careful student of the Word of God and the workings of God!

Personal Notes:

_____
_____
_____
_____
_____
_____
_____
_____
_____
_____
_____
_____
_____
_____
_____
_____
_____
_____
_____
_____
_____
_____
_____
_____
_____
_____
_____

Devotion 53

After the great victory over the kings and armies of Midian, the children of Israel made a huge offer to Gideon and his family:

Judges 8:22 *Then the men of Israel said unto Gideon, Rule thou over us, both thou, and thy son, and thy son's son also: for thou hast delivered us from the hand of Midian.*

They were offering to make Gideon a king and then let his son be king after that and then let his grandson be king after that. In other words, they were offering to establish a monarchy with the family of Gideon being the consistent and perpetual rulers for generation after generation to come. Gideon had proven himself, but neither his sons nor grandsons had done so. The children of Israel were making the mistake that so many people and nations have made through the years—ignoring merit in favor of heredity and familiarity. To his credit, Gideon turned that idea down flat:

Judges 8:23 *And Gideon said unto them, I will not rule over you, neither shall my son rule over you: the Lord shall rule over you.*

People make a major mistake when they base their decisions for leadership and other important issues on the things that they are familiar with alone: family, race, gender, friendship, social ties.

DO remember that God has taken many a person from an obscure background and gifted them with the ability to do great things. Never lock yourself into a "monarchy mentality," when God so often gives the greatest talents and abilities to "spiritual peasants!"

Personal Notes:

_____

_____

_____

_____

_____

_____

_____

_____

_____

_____

_____

_____

_____

_____

_____

_____

_____

_____

_____

_____

_____

_____

_____

_____

_____

_____

_____

Devotion 54

After turning down the children of Israel's offer to have him and his family establish a monarchy, Gideon did make one request of the nation, a request that they obliged:

Judges 8:24 *And Gideon said unto them, I would desire a request of you, that ye would give me every man the earrings of his prey. (For they had golden earrings, because they were Ishmaelites.)* **25** *And they answered, We will willingly give them. And they spread a garment, and did cast therein every man the earrings of his prey.* **26** *And the weight of the golden earrings that he requested was a thousand and seven hundred shekels of gold; beside ornaments, and collars, and purple raiment that was on the kings of Midian, and beside the chains that were about their camels' necks.*

The account of the mistake that Gideon made with this gold is for another day. Right now, what catches my attention is the fact that soldiers and even their camels were wearing golden earrings and chains and ornaments! They must have looked very pretty out there on the battlefield...but they lost. "Pretty" is never the issue; who is on the Lord's side is the issue!

And yet "Christianity" often devolves into a matter of who or what looks the best on the outside. Does that person draw a crowd of 10,000 and have a Colgate smile? He must be right. Has this person built a worldwide following on the internet? He must be right. But by that measure, when the battle began, the Midianites with all of their gold and all of their followers would have been the ones on the right side of the issue, and Gideon would have been the one on the wrong side of the issue! But you know better.

DO make up your mind to always evaluate people and ministries and situations not on the "glitter," but on the substance!

Personal Notes:

_____

_____

_____

_____

_____

_____

_____

_____

_____

_____

_____

_____

_____

_____

_____

_____

_____

_____

_____

_____

_____

_____

_____

_____

_____

_____

Devotion 55

For several chapters now in the book of Judges we have been observing the rule of Gideon, a great man who did great things for Israel. But as we come to the end of chapter eight, we see Israel going the way that they always went:

Judges 8:33 *And it came to pass, as soon as Gideon was dead, that the children of Israel turned again, and went a whoring after Baalim, and made Baal-berith their god.*

Forsaking Jehovah, the children of Israel begin to seek after a false God called Baal-berith. Baal-berith means "the god of the covenant." This was the "god" whose chief duty was to preside over compacts, treaties, promises, and covenants.

Do you see the incredible irony? The children of Israel were literally breaking their covenant with Jehovah so they could go and serve "the god of covenants." It would seem like the irony of that would jog their memories and make them realize how very foolish they were being. But people who are intent on not serving God tend to be very forgetful, intentionally so. They especially want to forget all of the promises that they themselves have made to serve God back when they were right with God.

Have you made promises to God somewhere along the way? Promises to serve Him, promises to be faithful, promises to give, promises to win souls, promises to live right? DO remember those covenants and keep them!

Personal Notes:

_____
_____
_____
_____
_____
_____
_____
_____
_____
_____
_____
_____
_____
_____
_____
_____
_____
_____
_____
_____
_____
_____
_____
_____
_____
_____
_____
_____

Devotion 56

Yesterday we observed that the children of Israel had intentionally forgotten their covenant with God and gone after a false God named Baal-berith. But, as is usually the case, when people choose to be forgetful about God, it never seems to stop there.

Judges 8:34 *And the children of Israel remembered not the Lord their God, who had delivered them out of the hands of all their enemies on every side:* **35** *Neither shewed they kindness to the house of Jerubbaal, namely, Gideon, according to all the goodness which he had shewed unto Israel.*

Having intentionally forgotten God, it was not much of a leap for them to move right from that to forgetting Gideon and all that he had done for them. And as we will see in the next chapter of the book of Judges, they turned on the house of Gideon and destroyed them all, after having proclaimed their undying love and devotion for them not too long before.

DO remember God, and DO also remember those who have served you on His behalf!

Personal Notes:

_____

_____

_____

_____

_____

_____

_____

_____

_____

_____

_____

_____

_____

_____

_____

_____

_____

_____

_____

_____

_____

_____

_____

_____

_____

_____

_____

Devotion 57

Judges nine is one of the saddest chapters in the Bible. One of the sons of Gideon, Abimelech, went to his mother's family in Shechem, and convinced them to help him kill all of his brothers, seventy young men. And they did, execution style, one by one. But not seventy; only sixty-nine. The youngest son, Jotham, managed to hide himself from the slaughter. Shortly thereafter he went into the mountain and shouted into the valley where his voice could be heard. He gave a parable about what Abimilech and the men of Shechem had done. And then once the parable was done, he gave the conclusion:

Judges 9:19 *If ye then have dealt truly and sincerely with Jerubbaal and with his house this day, then rejoice ye in Abimelech, and let him also rejoice in you:* **20** *But if not, let fire come out from Abimelech, and devour the men of Shechem, and the house of Millo; and let fire come out from the men of Shechem, and from the house of Millo, and devour Abimelech.*

These words of Jotham seemed like a pipe dream. He was ordering a curse that the people who had been confederate in destroying his family would turn on each other. What is the likelihood of that? After all, all of them had gotten what they wanted! And yet, that is exactly what happened by the end of the chapter. People who had done wickedly to someone else turned on each other and did wickedly to each other.

DO remember, as you go through your life and choose your friends, to choose them on the basis of righteousness, not on the basis of wickedness.

People who will do wrong FOR you will also do wrong TO you!

Personal Notes:

_____

_____

_____

_____

_____

_____

_____

_____

_____

_____

_____

_____

_____

_____

_____

_____

_____

_____

_____

_____

_____

_____

_____

_____

Devotion 58

Abimelech was still riding high after destroying his brothers and making himself king, but the curse of Jotham was going to begin to take affect very shortly. A man named Gaal, for some reason, got angry with Abimilech and begin to run his mouth about him. He was very "brave" in all of the things he said, and he said them where almost everyone could hear them—everyone but Abimilech, that is. Abimilech was nowhere around when this guy was proclaiming how he was going to tear him to pieces. A man named Zebul heard all of this and secretly told Abimilech, who promptly made his was there to confront Gaal. When Gaal and Zebul saw them coming, it is evident that Gaal suddenly got very scared and very quiet. We know this because of the words that Zebul then taunted him with:

Judges 9:38 *Then said Zebul unto him, Where is now thy mouth, wherewith thou saidst, Who is Abimelech, that we should serve him? is not this the people that thou hast despised? go out, I pray now, and fight with them.*

"Where is thy mouth" means "why have you stopped talking?" What a taunt! He had run his mouth when Abimilech was nowhere around, and now that Abimilech was here, he was being challenged to back up his big talk.

Does this have any application for us today? That question does not even really need to be asked in the day of "internet warriors," now does it… Every one of us need to be very careful not to be any "braver" online then we would actually be in person. People are getting notorious these days for running their mouths behind the anonymity of a computer screen, when, if they were ever confronted by the person they are blabbering about, they would probably be much more reserved!

DO Realize that every person you speak to online may eventually be a person that you have to face, face-to-face!

Personal Notes:

_____

_____

_____

_____

_____

_____

_____

_____

_____

_____

_____

_____

_____

_____

_____

_____

_____

_____

_____

_____

_____

_____

Devotion 59

It did not take long at all for Abimilech to be winning his fight with Gaal. But he did not stop with simply winning that fight; he determined to make an example out of a great many people, whether they were involved in it or not. He came against the city of Shechem to fight. Now, Zebul (who was on Abimilech's side) had already thrown Gaal out of the city. But that did not stop Abimilech from coming against the city anyway. Verse forty-five tells us that he beat down the city and sowed it with salt. He ruined it for years to come. And then we read this:

Judges 9:48 *And Abimelech gat him up to mount Zalmon, he and all the people that were with him; and Abimelech took an axe in his hand, and cut down a bough from the trees, and took it, and laid it on his shoulder, and said unto the people that were with him, What ye have seen me do, make haste, and do as I have done.* **49** *And all the people likewise cut down every man his bough, and followed Abimelech, and put them to the hold, and set the hold on fire upon them; so that all the men of the tower of Shechem died also, about a thousand men and women.*

Zebul sided with Abimilech, and as a reward for that his city was beaten down, ruined with salt for years to come, and the main tower was burned down with a thousand men and women inside it. We never hear of Zebul again after verse forty-one. Whether he lived or died, he was ruined, and he was ruined by the very man to whom he gave his loyalty.

DO give your loyalty to the righteous, never to the wicked. You may be loyal to the wicked, but the wicked will never truly be loyal to you, they will always only truly be loyal to themselves.

Personal Notes:

_____

_____

_____

_____

_____

_____

_____

_____

_____

_____

_____

_____

_____

_____

_____

_____

_____

_____

_____

_____

_____

_____

_____

_____

_____

_____

_____

Devotion 60

Abimilech was still riding high. All of his brothers were dead; he was in charge; his recent adversary, Gaal, had been defeated; the city of Shechem had fallen. So far, it seemed like only half of the curse of Jotham was coming to pass. But the other half of that curse was coming; and by the time it "hit him" it would be too late to repent.

Judges 9:52 *And Abimelech came unto the tower, and fought against it, and went hard unto the door of the tower to burn it with fire. 53 And a certain woman cast a piece of a millstone upon Abimelech's head, and all to brake his skull.*

Just like the city of Shechem, the city of Thebez, which he was now fighting against, had a tower. He intended to burn it down along with everyone inside it, just like he had done in Shechem. But this time one unnamed woman saved the day, and all it took for her to do so was gravity and a rock. Abimilech finally got what for a very long time had been coming to him. People seem to think that they will be the one to not be affected by the law of sowing and reaping, but there has never been such a person.

DO every single day sow a life that you will not mind reaping the consequences of!

Personal Notes:

_____

_____

_____

_____

_____

_____

_____

_____

_____

_____

_____

_____

_____

_____

_____

_____

_____

_____

_____

_____

_____

_____

_____

_____

_____

_____

Devotion 61

Abimilech was now dead, and a new judge arose over Israel.

Judges 10:1 *And after Abimelech there arose to defend Israel Tola the son of Puah, the son of Dodo, a man of Issachar; and he dwelt in Shamir in mount Ephraim.* **2** *And he judged Israel twenty and three years, and died, and was buried in Shamir.*

Whereas some judges had a great deal written and recorded about them, Tola has very little said about him. What little is said, though, is significant.

Tola judged Israel for twenty-three years. That was a relatively long time; this man was faithful. But we are also told that he defended Israel. He believed the country God had given him was special and worthy of being protected. There is very little that is more maddening than to see people in America, with all of the freedom and opportunity God has afforded us here, badmouth this nation. No nation ever has been or ever will be perfect. Israel was not perfect, especially during the time of the judges! But Tola defended his land, he loved his land, he was faithful to his land.

DO understand just how blessed we are here, and in gratitude to the God who gave us this land, defend it!

Personal Notes:

_____
_____
_____
_____
_____
_____
_____
_____
_____
_____
_____
_____
_____
_____
_____
_____
_____
_____
_____
_____
_____
_____
_____
_____
_____
_____
_____
_____
_____

Devotion 62

After the death of Tola, a judge named Jair rose to power. But after he was dead, the children of Israel turned evil again, and began to serve the same false gods that had gotten them into trouble over and over again already. Because of that, God gave them into the hands of the Philistines and the Ammonites. For eighteen years they suffered under that bondage, and finally they began to cry out unto the Lord, acknowledging their sin against Him in Judges 10:10. His answer to them was sharp:

Judges 10:14 *Go and cry unto the gods which ye have chosen; let them deliver you in the time of your tribulation.*

God had heard these words out of their mouths before. He really wasn't interested in hearing hollow words again. But in verse sixteen, the entire dynamic changed:

Judges 10:16 *And they put away the strange gods from among them, and served the Lord: and his soul was grieved for the misery of Israel.*

In verse ten they were saying "we are sorry." By verse sixteen they were doing more than "saying:" they were actually throwing out their sin. The saying did not get God's attention; the forsaking of sin did.

Many years ago, we had a gentleman come to the church who had a sin problem. Every few weeks, after having been out of church and openly involved in sin he would come back for a service, kneel down weeping at the altar, and then get up, turn to the congregation, and give a weeping testimony of how "he had returned, and this time it was for real." After several episodes of that, I intercepted him one Sunday as he got up from the altar and started to turn toward the congregation. I looked him in the eye and said, "no one really wants to hear it; everyone wants to see it. Just do right, consistently, and you won't have to say anything, everyone will know that it is real."

DO remember that talk really is cheap; DO right, and you won't have to talk much at all!

Personal Notes:

_____
_____
_____
_____
_____
_____
_____
_____
_____
_____
_____
_____
_____
_____
_____
_____
_____
_____
_____
_____
_____
_____
_____
_____

Devotion 63

At the end of chapter ten, Israel had cried out to God for mercy, but more importantly, they had forsaken their sin. Because of that, God began to raise up another judge to deliver them, a man with a less than stellar heritage, named Jephthah.

Judges 11:1 *Now Jephthah the Gileadite was a mighty man of valour, and he was the son of an harlot: and Gilead begat Jephthah.* **2** *And Gilead's wife bare him sons; and his wife's sons grew up, and they thrust out Jephthah, and said unto him, Thou shalt not inherit in our father's house; for thou art the son of a strange woman.*

As we are introduced to Jephthah, we find that his father had slept with a prostitute, resulting in Jephthah's conception. As the boy grew, his half brothers chased him away from home because of how he had been conceived. I think it is obvious to say that the boy had nothing to do with how he came to be. Therefore, it was entirely unfair and unkind to despise him and be cruel to him on those grounds.

Throughout our lives we will need to evaluate people for a variety of reasons; will they make a good employee, will they be a suitable mate, will they be a good friend? But one thing we should never do is hold things against people that were or are entirely out of their control.

DO be as fair to others based on uncontrollable things as you would want others to be to you over uncontrollable things!

Personal Notes:

_____

_____

_____

_____

_____

_____

_____

_____

_____

_____

_____

_____

_____

_____

_____

_____

_____

_____

_____

_____

_____

_____

_____

_____

Devotion 64

As we began to see the life of Jephthah unfold in our previous devotion, we found that his brothers chased him away from home over the uncontrollable circumstances of his conception. But in the process of time, the Ammonites went to war against Israel. It is then that the very people of Gilead, the people who had allowed the brothers of Jephthah to cast him out, went looking for him.

Judges 11:5 *And it was so, that when the children of Ammon made war against Israel, the elders of Gilead went to fetch Jephthah out of the land of Tob:*

Judges 11:1 lets us know that Jephthah was a brave man, a fighter. And so when the time to fight came, they went looking for him. But that says something about his brothers, does it not? If any of them had been brave, if any of them had been skillful fighters, there would have been no need to go looking for him! In other words, the people who so haughtily cast him out were themselves of very little value! In other words, they were too proud to learn from Jephthah. Their "pure blood" made them special, or so they imagined.

DO remember that one person's pedigree is of far less worth than another person's ability. It would be better for us to be effective people from nowhere than incompetent people from somewhere!

Personal Notes:

_____

_____

_____

_____

_____

_____

_____

_____

_____

_____

_____

_____

_____

_____

_____

_____

_____

_____

_____

_____

_____

_____

_____

_____

_____

Devotion 65

Jephthah was brought back, installed as the judge of Israel, and was now tasked with facing off against the Ammonites. In Judges 11:12 he sent messengers to the king of Ammon and asked him why he had come to fight against them. Here is the answer that the king of Ammon gave:

Judges 11:13 *And the king of the children of Ammon answered unto the messengers of Jephthah, Because Israel took away my land, when they came up out of Egypt, from Arnon even unto Jabbok, and unto Jordan: now therefore restore those lands again peaceably.*

So, we see that the claim was that Israel had taken away land from the Ammonites. Now look at Jephthah's response:

Judges 11:21 *And the Lord God of Israel delivered Sihon and all his people into the hand of Israel, and they smote them: so Israel possessed all the land of the Amorites, the inhabitants of that country.* **22** *And they possessed all the coasts of the Amorites, from Arnon even unto Jabbok, and from the wilderness even unto Jordan.* **23** *So now the Lord God of Israel hath dispossessed the Amorites from before his people Israel, and shouldest thou possess it?*

Many years ago, on Sesame Street a little song was sung which went, "one of these things is not like the other, one of these things is not the same…" Who was it, again that was currently coming against Israel? That would be he Ammonites. But in Jephthah's answer, what similar sounding but in actuality very different people does he say the land was taken from? That would be the Amorites. The Ammonites and

Amorites may sound similar, but they were two different nations! The king of the Ammonites was hoping Jephthah would not notice that. It is incredibly important, especially in these days when history is being rewritten, that all of us be very diligent students of history! In the case of Israel and Jephthah, had Jephthah not done his homework concerning events from three hundred years earlier, he may have been fooled by what he was being told. But since he was a good student of history, he did not buy the lie, not even for a second.

DO spend more time with history books than you do with Facebook or a fiction book or a comic book or any other book other than the Bible! A nation's future is dependent on people remembering their own history!

Personal Notes:

_____

_____

_____

_____

_____

_____

_____

_____

_____

_____

_____

_____

_____

_____

_____

_____

Devotion 66

As Jephthah continued his response to the king of the Ammonites, he got around to playing the "god card:"

Judges 11:24 *Wilt not thou possess that which Chemosh thy god giveth thee to possess? So whomsoever the Lord our God shall drive out from before us, them will we possess.*

This was both a statement of a well-established historical principle (the principle that whatever land people captured and held by conquest was theirs as long as they could hold it) and a theological challenge as well. Jephthah was basically throwing down the gauntlet and saying, "Why are you complaining to me about this? Is your Chemosh not powerful enough to give you the land? Will you not have whatever he gives you, while we have whatever our God gives us?" This was Jephthah's way of pointing out that not all belief systems are equal, and not all "gods" are equal. It is amazing that even today, thousands of years later, people fail to understand this!

DO remember that theological equivalency is illogical and unbiblical all at once. There can only be one true God, and the evidence says that we are serving that one true God!

Personal Notes:

Devotion 67

After the king of the Ammonites made it clear that he was going to come to war against Israel, Jephthah begin to prepare for the fight. Part of his preparation was a vow that he made to the Lord in Judges 11:30-31. The vow that he made was that whatever came out of the doors of his house to meet him after the battle, he would offer it up to the LORD for a burnt offering. If that sounds a bit vague, it was. And that ended up causing Jephthah a huge problem. When he came home successful from the battle, his daughter was the first thing that came out of the door to meet him. Notice what he said in verse thirty-five after this happened:

Judges 11:35 *And it came to pass, when he saw her, that he rent his clothes, and said, Alas, my daughter! thou hast brought me very low, and thou art one of them that trouble me: for I have opened my mouth unto the Lord , and I cannot go back.*

Jephthah's rash vow put him in an extreme moral conundrum. Would he offer his daughter as a burnt sacrifice, or would he go back on his vow to the Lord? In Jephthah's mind, either one of those things would have been a sin, but going back on his vow to the Lord, to him, would have been the bigger sin. And so, according to verse thirty-nine, he fulfilled his vow. Was he right or wrong? People have debated that for a very long time. But the answer is much simpler than you might imagine. Jephthah promised to do something that was clearly against the Word and the will of the God who had said, "Thou shall not kill," and who repeatedly told them never to let their children pass through the fire. He took the proud way

136

out, fulfilling a vow that he, in his carelessness, uttered rather than taking the humble way out and admitting that he had sinned by uttering a foolish vow. He did not fix a problem; he compounded a problem. He added murder to carelessness.

Whenever our own sin or carelessness puts us in a position where there are only bad options, we should always take the option that puts any harm on ourselves, never an option that puts any harm on others.

DO be careful to know the ramifications of any promise before you make that promise. And if you ever make a promise and later discover that fulfilling it will harm others, apologize for your carelessness, but never take whatever route will harm others, no matter what you have promised!

Personal Notes:

_____
_____
_____
_____
_____
_____
_____
_____
_____
_____
_____
_____
_____
_____
_____

Devotion 68

Imagine, if you will, a situation in which some of your friends tell you that someone was supposed to have called them and yet did not call them. Your friends are incredibly upset; they regard this as intentional and as an insult. They are hurt, and they are angry. How would you feel about whoever it is that slighted your friends in that manner?

In Judges 12:1, we find a situation in which people were very upset over not having been called:

Judges 12:1 *And the men of Ephraim gathered themselves together, and went northward, and said unto Jephthah, Wherefore passedst thou over to fight against the children of Ammon, and didst not call us to go with thee? we will burn thine house upon thee with fire.*

The men of Ephraim were so angry with Jephthah over not calling them to the battle that they determined to kill him and his entire family. But look, please, at the very next verse:

Judges 12:2 *And Jephthah said unto them, I and my people were at great strife with the children of Ammon; and when I called you, ye delivered me not out of their hands.*

In verse one they said, "You did not call us!" In verse two, though, he said, "I did call you!"

Now go back to our introductory question. How would you feel if you had gotten angry along with your friends, only later to find out that they were either accidentally or intentionally incorrect, and that they had been called? I imagine you would feel very foolish for having gotten dragged into something like that.

And yet that kind of thing happens all the time. People hear one side of a story, and they immediately think they know everything there is to know. It is called "assuming." Nothing good ever comes from assuming anything!

DO memorize and learn an incredibly helpful verse about assumptions: **Proverbs 18:13** *He that answereth a matter before he heareth it, it is folly and shame unto him.* A person who never "jumps" to conclusions never "lands" in the wrong place!

Personal Notes:

_____

_____

_____

_____

_____

_____

_____

_____

_____

_____

_____

_____

_____

_____

_____

_____

_____

_____

_____

_____

Devotion 69

The argument between Jephthah and the men of Ephraim ended up breaking out into a full scale battle. It ended up being a battle that Jephthah and the men of Gilead resoundingly won. The Ephraimites were quickly on the run and fleeing for their lives. In order to escape back to their territory, they had to cross the Jordan River. But Jephthah and the Gileadites got there first. Now, since they were all Israelites, just from different tribes, they all looked alike, and it isn't like they were wearing uniforms to distinguish who was on whose side. So, the men of Ephraim tried to escape by pretending they were Gileadites. But one small thing kept that from happening:

Judges 12:5 *And the Gileadites took the passages of Jordan before the Ephraimites: and it was so, that when those Ephraimites which were escaped said, Let me go over; that the men of Gilead said unto him, Art thou an Ephraimite? If he said, Nay;* **6** *Then said they unto him, Say now Shibboleth: and he said Sibboleth: for he could not frame to pronounce it right. Then they took him, and slew him at the passages of Jordan: and there fell at that time of the Ephraimites forty and two thousand.*

Just like people from different areas of our own country do not pronounce things quite the same way, people from one area of Israel did not pronounce things like people from other areas of Israel. In other words, they claimed to be one thing, but their speech gave them away as something else entirely.

I am amazed at how often people claim to be "Christians," but their speech betrays them as something else. Cursing, lewd jokes, violence and hatred, these things are not the marks and the words of a Christian! They are the marks and the words either of a lost person or a very backslidden believer.

Jesus said in **Matthew 12:37** *For by thy words thou shalt be justified, and by thy words thou shalt be condemned.*

DO keep your heart so pure that the words that come out of your mouth betray you as being a Christian not as being a heathen!

Personal Notes:

_____

_____

_____

_____

_____

_____

_____

_____

_____

_____

_____

_____

_____

_____

_____

_____

_____

_____

_____

_____

Devotion 70

Judges 13 begins the account of the most memorable of all of the judges of Israel, Samson. Samson's story started with his barren mother and father. An angel appeared to the woman and told her that she was going to give birth to a very special child who would be a Nazarite from his mother's womb and would begin to deliver Israel from the bondage of the Philistines.

When the angel delivered this message, the woman's husband was not there. Immediately, she came and told her husband what happened. Shortly thereafter the angel appeared to the woman again, in response to the man's prayer that he come back and speak to them, but once again, her husband was not there when the angel arrived. Look at what happened:

Judges 13:9 *And God hearkened to the voice of Manoah; and the angel of God came again unto the woman as she sat in the field: but Manoah her husband was not with her.* **10** *And the woman made haste, and ran, and shewed her husband, and said unto him, Behold, the man hath appeared unto me, that came unto me the other day.*

This woman ran immediately and told her husband. There is some incredible wisdom in that.

One of the things that I as a pastor have seen be so problematic in homes through the years is husbands and wives that keep secrets from each other. Not pleasant secrets like a gift that one is about to receive, or a special trip that has been set up as a surprise, but important information that both should be privy to.

142

Transparency is the ally of a good marriage. Husbands and wives who do not keep secrets from each other give and gain trust to and from each other. In general, marriages where there are no secrets have infinitely fewer problems than marriages where there are secrets.

DO be transparent with your spouse in all things. The best things grow in the sunlight, not in the darkness!

Personal Notes:

_____

_____

_____

_____

_____

_____

_____

_____

_____

_____

_____

_____

_____

_____

_____

_____

_____

_____

_____

_____

_____

_____

Devotion 71

As Manoah and his wife spoke to the angel about their son who would be born, Samson, they prepared a burnt offering for the Lord, not even knowing they were doing so in the presence of an angel. When they offered it in front of him, he stepped into the fire and ascended up into heaven in front of them! It was only then that they realized they had been in the presence of an angel. At that shocking moment, Manoah panicked:

Judges 13:22 *And Manoah said unto his wife, We shall surely die, because we have seen God.*

"We shall surely die! Aggghhhh!" But wait; that is not the end of the story. Manoah may have panicked, but fortunately, he had a very levelheaded wife:

Judges 13:23 *But his wife said unto him, If the Lord were pleased to kill us, he would not have received a burnt offering and a meat offering at our hands, neither would he have shewed us all these things, nor would as at this time have told us such things as these.*

Situations in life that are unfamiliar to us or that seem to hold the prospect of imminent disaster often scare us into a sense of panic. But Dana and I have developed a rule through the years that we have tried very hard to follow, a rule that has served us well: "never panic at the same time."

DO make a decision to always have at least one person in every situation who is not allowed to panic. If you cannot decide ahead of time who that gets to be, just make it a rule that whoever does not panic first does not get to panic at all!" Panic very rarely makes things better, in fact, it almost always makes things worse. The world has designated drivers; Christians ought to have "designated non-panickers!"

Personal Notes:

_____

_____

_____

_____

_____

_____

_____

_____

_____

_____

_____

_____

_____

_____

_____

_____

_____

_____

_____

_____

_____

_____

_____

_____

_____

Devotion 72

As Samson grew to adulthood, he began his famous slide into degeneracy. A man who had all of the potential in the world for God squandered it by chasing after the wrong kind of women. This lifestyle started for him in Judges 14:3.

Judges 14:3 *Then his father and his mother said unto him, Is there never a woman among the daughters of thy brethren, or among all my people, that thou goest to take a wife of the uncircumcised Philistines? And Samson said unto his father, Get her for me; for she pleaseth me well.*

Well before Samson ever got entangled with Delilah and got his famous haircut, he was already in the established habit of seeking after Philistine women. His parents had to ask him if there was a "never" a woman among the Israelites, a true believer in God, that he was interested in. Samson's answer to his father's inquiry was, "Get her for me; for she pleaseth me well." For Samson, the only thing that mattered was how attractive a woman was, how alluring she was, how she enticed his flesh. The spiritual was of no value to him; and as a result a life full of potential ended up as a wasted life full of regret.

You single folks, DO make up your mind now that while physical attraction is somewhat important, spirituality is utterly essential! Looks quickly fade; wickedness has the capacity to last forever and to destroy anyone foolish enough to get entangled with it!

Personal Notes:

_____

_____

_____

_____

_____

_____

_____

_____

_____

_____

_____

_____

_____

_____

_____

_____

_____

_____

_____

_____

_____

_____

_____

_____

_____

_____

_____

Devotion 73

After Samson made it clear that he was going to have his Philistine wife no matter what his parents thought about it, they all went down to Timmath to set up the wedding. But on the way there, something happened that was highly unusual in two distinct ways:

Judges 14:5 *Then went Samson down, and his father and his mother, to Timnath, and came to the vineyards of Timnath: and, behold, a young lion roared against him.* **6** *And the Spirit of the Lord came mightily upon him, and he rent him as he would have rent a kid, and he had nothing in his hand: but he told not his father or his mother what he had done.*

The first and most obvious thing that is unusual about this is that Samson killed a lion with his bare hands. But the less obvious yet more unusual thing about it is that Samson very specifically did not tell his parents about his great victory. In fact, it seems that he told no one at all! If someone today killed a lion with their bare hands, it would be trending on Twitter within the hour, and the video would go viral.

Why did Samson, a very egotistical man, keep so very quiet about this? Because, as the very next verse makes clear, he was focused on fulfilling the desire of his flesh. If he had told his parents what happened, they surely would have pointed out to Samson that God had raised and prepared and equipped him for a high spiritual calling, and he was throwing that calling away. Samson kept quiet because he did not want any spiritual people bothering him with reminders that he, too, was supposed to be spiritual.

God is very good about bringing reminders into our lives. DO heed those reminders! They may make us uncomfortable, but conviction usually does. But reminders heeded could have saved Samson untold trouble and can do the same for us.

Personal Notes:

_____

_____

_____

_____

_____

_____

_____

_____

_____

_____

_____

_____

_____

_____

_____

_____

_____

_____

_____

_____

_____

_____

_____

_____

_____

Devotion 74

During the days of the wedding feast, Samson was interacting with the Philistines. Here is how that went:

Judges 14:12 *And Samson said unto them, I will now put forth a riddle unto you: if ye can certainly declare it me within the seven days of the feast, and find it out, then I will give you thirty sheets and thirty change of garments:* **13** *But if ye cannot declare it me, then shall ye give me thirty sheets and thirty change of garments. And they said unto him, Put forth thy riddle, that we may hear it.*

Riddles. Gambling. Samson was literally playing games with the Philistines. The problem is, he was not raised and empowered by God to play games with the Philistines; he was raised and empowered by God to battle the Philistines. Samson had gotten so very comfortable in Philistine territory and around the Philistine ways and values that he was socially acceptable to them, and they were socially acceptable to him.

We are in the world... but we are not of the world. All through Scripture God calls us to be separate and distinct. Yet people today carry the name Christian all the while fitting in with sinners. Samson as a Jew in Philistine territory playing games with the Philistines was neither a testimony to the Philistines nor a leader to the Jews.

DO make up your mind to be salt and light to this world, not sugar and sunglasses. Let the world see that you stand for righteousness, and let God's people be able to follow you as you do!

Personal Notes:

_____

_____

_____

_____

_____

_____

_____

_____

_____

_____

_____

_____

_____

_____

_____

_____

_____

_____

_____

_____

_____

_____

_____

_____

_____

_____

_____

Devotion 75

Samson gave his riddle to his Philistine friends, and it was a doozy. After days and days of trying to figure it out, they finally decided to cheat. They told his wife, one of their own people, that if she did not get the answer from Samson and give it to them they would burn her and her father's house to the ground with them inside it. So, Samson's wife pleaded with him to tell her the answer to the riddle. His answer to her, to say the very least, knocked him out of the running for the "husband of the year" award:

Judges 14:16 A*nd Samson's wife wept before him, and said, Thou dost but hate me, and lovest me not: thou hast put forth a riddle unto the children of my people, and hast not told it me. And he said unto her, Behold, I have not told it my father nor my mother, and shall I tell it thee?*

"I have not told it to daddy or mama; do you expect me to tell you?" Nice work there, Samson, way to win a wife's heart...

But this has always been an issue among some from age to age. Many people actually get married without any intention to put their spouse first, even over parents. If everything is done right, marriage is addition, not subtraction. A man and a woman add one family to another family, and everyone maintains good relationships all the way around. But when a marriage takes place, that spouse must immediately take priority. Samson showed poor husband skills, and his marriage suffered for it.

DO examine your people priority list and make sure that your spouse has first place. And if you are single yet unwilling to give a potential spouse first place once you say, "I do," then you are not yet ready to say, "I do!"

Personal Notes:

_____

_____

_____

_____

_____

_____

_____

_____

_____

_____

_____

_____

_____

_____

_____

_____

_____

_____

_____

_____

_____

_____

_____

_____

_____

Devotion 76

Samson had refused to tell his wife the answer to the riddle. In a classic bit of poor husbanding, he said, "I haven't even told my dad or mom; what makes you think I would tell you?!?" But that wasn't the end of the story:

Judges 14:17 *And she wept before him the seven days, while their feast lasted: and it came to pass on the seventh day, that he told her, because she lay sore upon him: and she told the riddle to the children of her people.*

Samson was determined not to tell her. And yet, the strongest man in history had the information pried out of him by a woman. She was infinitely weaker than him, yet by consistent emotional pressure she got it out of him. If that sounds familiar, it is because that is the very same way that Delilah later got the information that she wanted out of him! The strongest man physically was no match for emotional manipulation, because he was as weak in his walk with the Lord as he was strong in his body.

Physical health and strength is very valuable; but it does not hold a candle to spiritual strength. DO *"exercise yourself unto godliness"* as **1 Timothy 4:7** says. The devil and the world would love to wear you down by emotional manipulation, drawing you into all manner of sin; being spiritually strong will make that very unlikely to ever happen!

Personal Notes:

_____
_____
_____
_____
_____
_____
_____
_____
_____
_____
_____
_____
_____
_____
_____
_____
_____
_____
_____
_____
_____
_____
_____
_____
_____
_____

Devotion 77

Samson's wife emotionally manipulated him and got him to tell her the answer to his riddle. She then passed that information on to her Philistine friends, who smugly repeated the answer back to Samson and won the bet. Samson knew what had happened, and he was utterly livid. So he determined to pay the bet by taking it out of Philistine hides:

Judges 14:19 *And the Spirit of the Lord came upon him, and he went down to Ashkelon, and slew thirty men of them, and took their spoil, and gave change of garments unto them which expounded the riddle. And his anger was kindled, and he went up to his father's house.*

The fact that Samson slew those Philistines was not the issue; the Philistines were the brutal conquerors of His people, and God raised him up as a deliverer. The issue in this case was how Samson handled a marital problem. He and his wife were at odds, and he handled it by blowing up and leaving. That choice was the final nail in the coffin to his home; while he was gone, her father married her off to someone else.

Marriage often has problems arise between husband and wife. Spouses do not always see eye to eye. But blowing up and leaving is not the answer!

DO make up your mind to treasure the home you have been given enough to stay and fix things. Samson in his lifetime had many wicked lovers, but only one actual wife, and he destroyed his home by blowing up and leaving in a fit of rage.

Personal Notes:

Devotion 78

In Judges 14, Samson stormed away from his wife and went back home to his parents. After a while, though, the "call of the flesh" started working on him, and he decided to go back. But when he got there he found out that his wife was now someone else's wife! This was horribly wrong; it was wicked to the core. But look at how Samson responded:

Judges 15:3 *And Samson said concerning them, Now shall I be more blameless than the Philistines, though I do them a displeasure.*

Long story short, he determined to do great wrong to the Philistines to pay them back for the great wrong they had done to him. But what is truly fascinating is how he soothes his conscience over this: by comparing himself to them. He did not compare what he was about to do to how his parents behaved, or how some hero of the faith like Moses or Joshua behaved. He compared it to the behavior of the most wicked people around, the Philistines.

If we have to compare ourselves to reprobates to make ourselves comfortable with our own behavior, then our own behavior is wrong! DO determine that, if you ever compare your behavior or choices to others, you only use the most godly of people to compare against. Use comparisons that spur you on to greater holiness, never comparisons that make you feel comfortable with greater wickedness!

Personal Notes:

_____
_____
_____
_____
_____
_____
_____
_____
_____
_____
_____
_____
_____
_____
_____
_____
_____
_____
_____
_____
_____
_____
_____
_____
_____
_____
_____
_____
_____
_____

Devotion 79

Samson's wife and her father were dead, and the feud between him and the Philistines was heating up. After a couple more confrontations, an all out battle broke out between him, the strongest man who ever lived, and a huge company of them.

Judges 15:15 *And he found a new jawbone of an ass, and put forth his hand, and took it, and slew a thousand men therewith.* **16** *And Samson said, With the jawbone of an ass, heaps upon heaps, with the jaw of an ass have I slain a thousand men.*

Much preaching has been done through the years about the jawbone and what it spirituality typifies. But, laying aside the thought of a type, what we literally have is a man who picked up a weapon to fight with.

Think about that; the strongest man who ever lived recognized that his strength was not infinite. Whether we are talking about physical or spiritual or emotional, none of us have infinite strength. And that is why it is so important for us to humbly acknowledge our own weaknesses.

DO be willing to be honest, especially before the Lord and yourself and your spouse, about your weaknesses. The same God who provided the jawbone of an ass for Samson can provide us the assistance we need as well, but usually only if we are willing to be humble enough to reach out and take it!

Personal Notes:

_____
_____
_____
_____
_____
_____
_____
_____
_____
_____
_____
_____
_____
_____
_____
_____
_____
_____
_____
_____
_____
_____
_____
_____
_____
_____
_____

Devotion 80

As we continue in the life of Samson, we come to a very unflinching portrait of his wickedness:

Judges 16:1 *Then went Samson to Gaza, and saw there an harlot, and went in unto her.*

A harlot. A prostitute. Samson was living horribly wicked, and the Bible did not gloss over it in the slightest. The late Harold Wilmington once said, "The Bible is not a book that man would write if he could or could write if he would." He was talking about the very type of thing I just showed you.

All of the great heroes of the faith are shown in all of their failings, in all of the embarrassing details! The Bible is utterly honest about its "great men," because its great men did not author it; God did.

DO understand that this sets the Bible apart from other "holy books" which paint a superhuman portrait of their heroes. Books written by men for men do that; the one book written by God for men does not!

Personal Notes:

_____
_____
_____
_____
_____
_____
_____
_____
_____
_____
_____
_____
_____
_____
_____
_____
_____
_____
_____
_____
_____
_____
_____
_____
_____
_____

Devotion 81

As we progress through the life of Samson, it is inevitable that we finally come upon his downfall; a little woman named Delilah. Her name means "feeble," yet she was anything but. She was potent poison in pretty packaging.

Judges 16:6 *And Delilah said to Samson, Tell me, I pray thee, wherein thy great strength lieth, and wherewith thou mightest be bound to afflict thee.*

I am always amazed, each time I read this, at how utterly honest she was with Samson. You would think she would be deceptive and claim to have only his best interests at heart, but she came out openly and told him, from the start, that she wanted to know how to "bind and afflict" him!

How is it that Samson did not run screaming from the house and never return? Most men, if a woman said, "Hey, baby, how exactly could I torture and kill you?" would run screaming like a banshee trying to get as far away as possible from the psychopath! But you see, Samson had already been sleeping with Delilah. He was therefore not thinking clearly.

Fornication robs a person of their clarity of thought and makes them so very vulnerable to the devil's wiles that, even when the coming bitter end is obvious, they continue to stay in the very situation that is going to destroy them. Man or woman, DO heed God's command on intimacy; it is for a man and his wife, period, only, no exceptions. If you value your ability to think clearly, and if you desire to avoid disaster, never ever violate this command!

Personal Notes:

_____

_____

_____

_____

_____

_____

_____

_____

_____

_____

_____

_____

_____

_____

_____

_____

_____

_____

_____

_____

_____

_____

_____

_____

_____

_____

_____

_____

_____

Devotion 82

As Delilah continued to wear Samson down, we come to one of the saddest verses you will ever read:

Judges 16:15 *And she said unto him, How canst thou say, I love thee, when thine heart is not with me? thou hast mocked me these three times, and hast not told me wherein thy great strength lieth.*

Samson, the strongest man who ever lived, was telling Delilah that he loved her. She was openly trying to kill him, and he was telling her that he loved her. Needless to say, this was a decidedly "one way street." Delilah was lovely, but she was not loving. Samson was a business transaction to her, nothing more.

Parents, can you imagine seeing your child get caught up in a situation like this? And yet it is only all too possible for that very thing to happen. The devil has the wrong kind of boys and the wrong kind of girls just waiting in the wings to steal the hearts of our children.

DO pray for your children each and every day in regard to their future. DO fast for them. DO teach them what to look for and what to look out for. Don't spend eighteen to twenty years raising them only to see them taken in by a wicked emotional manipulator. Intercede for them as if their lives depend on it; they do!

Personal Notes:

_____
_____
_____
_____
_____
_____
_____
_____
_____
_____
_____
_____
_____
_____
_____
_____
_____
_____
_____
_____
_____
_____
_____
_____
_____

Devotion 83

If you were to ask people "who was the first person to ever cause Samson physical pain," most of them would probably answer, "whoever put his eyes out." But look at what the Bible says:

Judges 16:19 *And she made him sleep upon her knees; and she called for a man, and she caused him to shave off the seven locks of his head; and she began to afflict him, and his strength went from him.*

She. Delilah. SHE began to afflict him! The first pain that Samson ever felt was at the hands of Delilah, the one who won his heart, wheedled his secrets out of him, and sold him out to his enemies for money. What a horrible realization that must have been for Samson.

But give Delilah credit where it is due; out of the two of them, she is the one who never forgot who she was or what her purpose was! Had Samson not forgotten who he was or what his purpose was, he would never have laid his head in her lap to begin with! She was successful and he was a failure because she never forgot who she was or what her purpose was, and he did.

If you are saved, DO always remember who you are and what your purpose is. As Revelation 4:11 makes abundantly clear, the purpose of a child of God is to please God! Anything we do great or small that displeases Him is an example of us going the way of Samson and forgetting who we are and what our purpose is. And if Samson with all of his great strength could not do that without eventually being destroyed, it is safe to assume that none of us can either!

Personal Notes:

_____
_____
_____
_____
_____
_____
_____
_____
_____
_____
_____
_____
_____
_____
_____
_____
_____
_____
_____
_____
_____
_____
_____
_____
_____

Devotion 84

As Delilah began to afflict Samson, the Bible utters a heart-wrenching condemnation against this man who had been blessed with such God-given potential:

Judges 16:20 A*nd she said, The Philistines be upon thee, Samson. And he awoke out of his sleep, and said, I will go out as at other times before, and shake myself. And he wist not that the Lord was departed from him.*

He wist not means "he did not know." The presence of God was gone from his life, and he did not know it. He had been dabbling in sin and pushing God away for so long that God finally left him without him even realizing it. How sad that something that significant could happen and a person not even realize it!

And yet, something very similar is still possible even for a child of God today. We are not guaranteed the power of God in our lives, none of us. The same thing that robbed Samson of God's presence can rob us of His power, and the outcome will be much the same: the ruin of a life.

DO walk so close to God that this never becomes an issue. The farther one walks from God, the easier it is to lose His power and favor and not even realize it has happened!

Personal Notes:

_____

_____

_____

_____

_____

_____

_____

_____

_____

_____

_____

_____

_____

_____

_____

_____

_____

_____

_____

_____

_____

_____

_____

_____

Devotion 85

Samson had been a powerful man throughout his life, able to do whatever he wanted whenever he wanted. Lift tons of weight worth of city gates? No sweat. Kill a lion with his bare hands? Done. But all of his strength was not actually his strength; it was the power of God. But after years of disobedience, that power was given away by Samson as he broke the very last of his Nazarite vows. His eyes were put out, and he became in his own words "like any other man." But he soon found out that even though God's power was gone, the need for strength was not.

Judges 16:21 *But the Philistines took him, and put out his eyes, and brought him down to Gaza, and bound him with fetters of brass; and he did grind in the prison house.*

Samson was awakened day after day, hooked to a grinding wheel, and made to push it around in circle after circle grinding grain. It was now his back and his legs and his arms that felt the strain. For the first time in his life he had to struggle and grunt and groan as he attempted to move a weight. His muscles got sore, his back doubtless experienced spasms, he got cramps. The power was gone; the weight still remained.

DO realize how very precious the power of God is on a life and never do anything to lose it! The weight of life will never go away when the power of God goes away; it will just fall on shoulders that have to struggle ineffectively in their own strength to lift it.

Personal Notes:

Devotion 86

As Samson worked at the grinding wheel in in the prison house of the Philistines, there came a day when they decided to have some fun with him. They gathered everyone together to have a great sacrifice to their god, Dagon, and brought out Samson to mock and make fun of as they did. But something they said as they did so is very instructive:

Judges 16:24 *And when the people saw him, they praised their god: for they said, Our god hath delivered into our hands our enemy, and the destroyer of our country, which slew many of us.*

Notice that they called Samson "our enemy." Throughout his life he made a habit of making friends; but always with the Philistines. He was supposed to be their enemy; after all, they had subjugated his people and were keeping them under bondage his entire lifetime. But while they had the wisdom to regard him as an enemy, he never had the same wisdom concerning them.

DO realize that a child of God has actual enemies. Whatever or whoever actively seeks to draw you into wickedness is not your friend! And in the end, no matter how "friendly" you were with it or them, the result will be your own destruction, and celebration on the part of your enemy.

Personal Notes:

_____

_____

_____

_____

_____

_____

_____

_____

_____

_____

_____

_____

_____

_____

_____

_____

_____

_____

_____

_____

_____

_____

_____

_____

_____

_____

_____

Devotion 87

As the Philistines mocked and made fun of Samson, they did not pay attention to the fact that his hair was growing again. And, while his God rather than his hair was the actual source of his strength, the Philistines seemed to overlook both his hair and his God. Samson, though, had finally gotten "blind enough to see." With his eyes gone he could no longer see all of the Philistine women that had so often allured him to sin. What he could see, by faith, was that there was still a God in heaven waiting to hear from him:

Judges 16:28 *And Samson called unto the Lord, and said, O Lord God, remember me, I pray thee, and strengthen me, I pray thee, only this once, O God, that I may be at once avenged of the Philistines for my two eyes.*

Samson prayed. What makes this so poignant is that in all of his life this is only the second time we see him doing so. And yet both times God answered and gave him the strength he needed. How sad is it that he only prayed twice; but how thrilling is it that God heard and answered both times!

No matter how weak and sporadic your prayer life has been, DO understand how very thrilled God is to have you come before Him in prayer! So, pray, child of God. Pray for the lost, pray for your spouse, pray for your children, pray for your church, pray for your leaders, pray for forgiveness, pray for your needs, pray just to be talking with the Creator who made you... Pray!

Personal Notes:

_____

_____

_____

_____

_____

_____

_____

_____

_____

_____

_____

_____

_____

_____

_____

_____

_____

_____

_____

_____

_____

_____

_____

_____

_____

_____

_____

_____

Devotion 88

As the Philistines mocked Samson, he prepared for one final act; but what a final act! With both his hair and his strength returning, the one thing Samson still did not have was the eyesight to know how to apply that strength. But that need was supplied from the unlikeliest of places: the Philistines themselves. A young man of the Philistines led Samson to the two center posts of the great assembly house. The entire weight of the structure rested on those posts. Samson leaned into them to topple the whole structure. But just before he did he said some of the saddest and most needless words ever spoken:

Judges 16:30 *And Samson said, Let me die with the Philistines. And he bowed himself with all his might; and the house fell upon the lords, and upon all the people that were therein. So the dead which he slew at his death were more than they which he slew in his life.*

Let me die with the Philistines. Those were words that never should have needed to be said. Had Samson lived like he was supposed to live, he would never have died like he died. It was the choices made within his life that dictated the horrible end of his life.

Variations of that scene happen every day all these thousands of years later. People who could have died surrounded by family and the family of God, leaving behind a legacy of godliness for their children and grandchildren to follow, instead die bitter and wasted, leaving nothing but the ashes of a life burned out by wickedness, worldliness, and wastefulness.

DO, every day of your life, live that life in such a way that when you are laying on your deathbed you can say, "I lived for the Lord!" rather than, "Let me die with the Philistines."

Personal Notes:

_____

_____

_____

_____

_____

_____

_____

_____

_____

_____

_____

_____

_____

_____

_____

_____

_____

_____

_____

_____

_____

_____

_____

_____

_____

Devotion 89

Samson was dead, but he was not forgotten.

Judges 16:31 *Then his brethren and all the house of his father came down, and took him, and brought him up, and buried him between Zorah and Eshtaol in the buryingplace of Manoah his father. And he judged Israel twenty years.*

His family came into Philistine territory, dug through the rubble, found his body, and brought him home. But one person was not there to bury him. You see, his father had already died. Samson's body was taken and buried alongside his father. Samson, in the last moments of his life, got right with God. But one person who died without ever seeing him get right was his father.

Many people have been prayed for, often for many years, by mothers and fathers and grandmothers and grandfathers. And yet oftentimes those prayer warriors go to the grave without seeing their prayers answered. God loves to see His children get right. But so do others!

If there is anything in your life separating you from a close fellowship with God, DO make it right sooner rather than later. Never let those you love go to their graves carrying unanswered prayers with them!

Personal Notes:

_____
_____
_____
_____
_____
_____
_____
_____
_____
_____
_____
_____
_____
_____
_____
_____
_____
_____
_____
_____
_____
_____
_____
_____
_____
_____

Devotion 90

As Judges 17 begins, Samson is dead, and the people are continuing their slide into sin. And yet, we find that it is not a whole-hearted rejection of God that we are dealing with, but a sad and in some ways almost humorous mixture of truth and error. Chapter seventeen begins the story of a man named Micah. According to verse five this man had a "house of gods." He was an idolater, but he also had an ephod, a priestly garment! Those two things most decidedly do not go together. He was also, according to verse two, a thief. And it was his own mother from whom he had stolen! He pilfered 1,100 shekels of silver from her.

And how did this "godly" mother respond? Not knowing who took the money, she cursed. And she cursed in the hearing of her own son. Can you imagine a mother being so wicked as to curse in front of her children? Micah, apparently feeling guilty, confessed to what he had done, and restored the silver to his mother. When he did, his mother responded, *"Blessed be thou of the LORD, my son."*

One moment she is cursing; the very next moment she is praising God and invoking the name of Jehovah. That is inconsistency of the most dramatic order. Is it any wonder she managed to produce a son who was just as inconsistent as she was in spiritual matters?

All of us, especially those of us who are parents and grandparents, have a great responsibility not just to be godly, but to be consistent in that godliness. DO determine that no matter when or under what circumstances your children or grandchildren see you, they always see you the exact same way, consistently living for the Lord!

Personal Notes:

_____

_____

_____

_____

_____

_____

_____

_____

_____

_____

_____

_____

_____

_____

_____

_____

_____

_____

_____

_____

_____

_____

_____

_____

_____

_____

_____

_____

Devotion 91

Immediately after we read about the house of gods of Micah, we come across the verse that gives us the root cause of all of the evil we find during the time period of the judges:

Judges 17:6 *In those days there was no king in Israel, but every man did that which was right in his own eyes.*

This is mentioned not just here in the book of Judges, but also in chapter twenty-one. Twice we are informed that everyone did what was right in their own eyes. This is the exact thing that Moses warned the people against back in Deuteronomy at 12:8. And yet it is also the exact thing that has our country, and even many once godly homes within our country, in the sorry state in which we currently find them.

The absolute allegiance to the Word of God as the authority for our lives is gone, and the result will always be turmoil and wickedness and judgment. But it is absolutely not necessary for it to be that way.

No matter what time we live in, no matter what the circumstances of the society around us, every one of us can and must choose to do what is right in God's eyes, not our own. DO determine to look at everything through God's eyes, and to see things the way that He sees them! Seeing things the way that He sees them will result in us doing things the way that He wants us to do them, and will bring the blessings of God in our lives that only come from obedience.

Personal Notes:

_____
_____
_____
_____
_____
_____
_____
_____
_____
_____
_____
_____
_____
_____
_____
_____
_____
_____
_____
_____
_____
_____
_____
_____

Devotion 92

As Micah was going about his daily business, a young man came traveling through. Micah asked the young man who he was, and the young man informed him that he was a Levite and was trying to find a place to live. Immediately Micah had an offer for him: come live with me and be a priest to my family. The young man quickly agreed to do so. Verse thirteen tells us why Micah was so very thrilled with that arrangement:

Judges 17:13 *Then said Micah, Now know I that the Lord will do me good, seeing I have a Levite to my priest.*

Please remember that this man was an idolater; he had a house full of false gods. And yet he is now convinced that God is going to bless him simply because he has a Levite as his priest. He is under the assumption that the perceived righteousness of someone else as his man of God will cause God to bless him despite his own aberrant behavior.

God's blessings do not come on our lives based on who our man of God is in exclusion to the actual behavior of our lives! Yes, it is important to have a good man of God in your life, but that will not make one ounce of difference to God if the behavior of our lives is contrary to the expectations of God's word.

DO carefully choose what man of God you will sit under and learn from, but be just as careful and even more so of the actual behavior of your life, because it is on that basis that God will bless you or chastise you, not the basis of who your preacher is.

Personal Notes:

_____

_____

_____

_____

_____

_____

_____

_____

_____

_____

_____

_____

_____

_____

_____

_____

_____

_____

_____

_____

_____

_____

_____

_____

_____

_____

_____

_____

Devotion 93

As the account of Micah and the Levite continued into chapter eighteen, five men from the tribe of Dan came through and lodged in Micah's house. It just so happened that they knew the young man, the Levite who had become the priest to Micah's family. These young men were on a scouting mission, gathering information to bring back to their tribe about a military conquest that they were going to engage in. When they realized the Levite was there, they decided to get something very important from him:

Judges 18:5 *And they said unto him, Ask counsel, we pray thee, of God, that we may know whether our way which we go shall be prosperous.*

These men wanted counsel of God; that is very good. But notice that they very specifically wanted to know whether the way that they were going to go would be "prosperous." There was a man of God in residence, and yet they did not ask him for counsel from God about their behavior or their salvation; they asked about earthly success.

That exact philosophy is at the heart of today's "prosperity gospel." Some of the most well-known "ministers" in our day are people who have made hundreds of millions of dollars by telling other people that God wants them to be wealthy and prosperous. No one seems to notice that the only ones actually getting wealthy and prosperous are the ministers themselves, while their followers get bilked out of bill money and their life's savings.

There was nothing truly godly about the request of these men from the Levite, and there is also nothing biblical or godly or even logical about the modern prosperity gospel. God did not come to fatten our wallets; He came to save our wretched souls and to make us useful in His service.

DO make up your mind never to view God as a genie in a bottle there to do your bidding and grant you goodies. He is the King of kings, the Lord of lords and deserves our reverence as such!

Personal Notes:

_____

_____

_____

_____

_____

_____

_____

_____

_____

_____

_____

_____

_____

_____

_____

_____

_____

_____

_____

_____

_____

_____

Devotion 94

After the five scouts left the house of Micah, they came to the city of Laish to spy it out and see if it could be conquered. They found exactly what they hoped to see:

Judges 18:7 *Then the five men departed, and came to Laish, and saw the people that were therein, how they dwelt careless, after the manner of the Zidonians, quiet and secure; and there was no magistrate in the land, that might put them to shame in any thing; and they were far from the Zidonians, and had no business with any man.*

These people were isolated and careless; they thought they would be able to live peacefully forever without any preparations for their own security. How could people possibly think such an illogical thing? The answer to that question is found in a phrase in verse seven that lets us know the true interest of these people. It says that *"there was no magistrate in the land, that might put them to shame in anything."* These people had put together a political system in which no one was allowed to be over them telling them that anything they were ever doing was wrong. They could sin at will, absolutely anything their flesh desired, and there would never be the convicting presence of anyone at all telling them that they needed to change their ways. They had achieved a liberal utopia. But as they were to shortly learn, every liberal utopia is simply a low hanging fruit ripe for the picking of enemies.

We can pray over and fast over our land, and be brokenhearted over the sin within it, and we should. But every land is made up of individual people. And in every individual heart there is always the rebellious desire to do whatever we want to do and have no one be allowed to tell us that it is wrong. But despite the fact that our flesh does not like it, some things are right, and some things are wrong. The most merciful thing anyone can ever do for us is put us to shame when we are doing wrong!

No one ever put the city of Laish to shame for any of their behavior. The result was that they quickly and easily fell before their enemies.

If no one is ever allowed to put us to shame, we will likewise quickly and easily fall before our adversary, the devil. DO Recognize that though rebuke for sin is not pleasant to us, it is actually far more beneficial to us than a situation in which we can do whatever we want to do without anyone making us feel shame over it.

Personal Notes:

_____

_____

_____

_____

_____

_____

_____

_____

_____

_____

_____

_____

_____

_____

_____

Devotion 95

The book of Judges marks the low point in the behavior of Israel in the Old Testament. But chapter nineteen marks the very lowest spot by far. It is a sordid series of events that leaves a person shaking their head and thinking, "It has to get better from here; there is nowhere lower to go!"

Verse two starts things off with a woman committing adultery, then running home to her father. The man went to talk her into coming home, and she agreed. They stopped over in Gibeah and lodged with a man. While he was there things continued on their down hill slide when in verse twenty-two a group of pervert men surrounded the house and demanded to be allowed to commit the vilest of acts against the man who had come to lodge there. Things got worse still when the owner of the house offered his own daughter and the man's concubine to them instead. Then the man sent his concubine out to them, and the result was unspeakable. The woman ended up dead.

End of the horrible story? Not quite. The man severed her body into twelve pieces and mailed each tribe of Israel one of the pieces as a message of what had happened. Now you see why this is the lowest of the low points in the entire Old Testament history of Israel's behavior.

But God is so good to allow us one gleam of hope as the tale comes to an end. The last phrase of verse thirty says, "Speak your minds." That phrase means, "Speak up and speak out about this!" When people saw what had happened, the response was to speak up. Silence was not an option. Sweeping things under the rug simply was not acceptable. In the face of evil, it never is!

Child of God, DO look around you. In the face of the evil in our own society, speak up and speak out! When babies are at risk in the very wombs of their mothers, speak up and speak out! When women are mistreated by cruel men, speak up and speak out! When lies are told about good people, speak up and speak out! When God is mocked, speak up and speak out! Evil is never defeated by silence. Whatever evil you are confronted by, speak up and speak out!

Personal Notes:

_____

_____

_____

_____

_____

_____

_____

_____

_____

_____

_____

_____

_____

_____

_____

_____

_____

_____

_____

_____

Devotion 96

After the debauchery and wickedness found in Judges 20, the children of Israel were awakened out of their spiritual slumber and once again motivated toward righteousness. The entire nation was gathered together as one man ready to stand and deliver judgment against the tribe of Benjamin, for it was their people who committed the great sin against the woman that resulted in her death.

And to war they went. One would suspect that after years of spiritual lethargy and moral apathy they would have no determination in the battle. But we find, to the contrary, that despite two initial severe losses, they persisted in the fight. By the time the battle was over we read of the decimation of Benjamin:

Judges 20:47 *But six hundred men turned and fled to the wilderness unto the rock Rimmon, and abode in the rock Rimmon four months.*

The entire tribe was reduced to just six hundred men. Their sin and the resulting judgment led to them nearly becoming extinct.

Sin, which so often promises the moon and delivers the pit instead, had done so once again. DO be determined never to be fooled by the glittery promises of unrighteousness. The devil is deceptive enough to offer things that are sure to allure us, great promises of advancement and popularity and wealth and pleasure, but whoever takes what he offers always finds out in the end that they have lost what they had rather than gained what they sought.

Personal Notes:

_____
_____
_____
_____
_____
_____
_____
_____
_____
_____
_____
_____
_____
_____
_____
_____
_____
_____
_____
_____
_____
_____
_____
_____
_____
_____
_____
_____

Devotion 97

By the time Judges 20 was done, the wickedness of the tribe of Benjamin had been punished. The result was that there were only six hundred men left out of the entire tribe and no wives for any of them. A tribe of Israel, one of the twelve, was at risk of becoming completely extinct. But to complicate matters even further, verse one of chapter twenty-one tells us that before they went to war with them, the rest of the tribes of Israel had sworn not to give any of their own daughters to any remaining man of Benjamin to marry! They had boxed themselves in with no way out.

But never fear; these tribes of Israel had a handy tool at their disposal to get around their self induced problem: A wink and a nudge.

Judges 21:20 *Therefore they commanded the children of Benjamin, saying, Go and lie in wait in the vineyards;* **21** *And see, and, behold, if the daughters of Shiloh come out to dance in dances, then come ye out of the vineyards, and catch you every man his wife of the daughters of Shiloh, and go to the land of Benjamin.*

These men who had promised that they would not "give" any of their daughters as wives to the Benjamites, settled for setting up a situation in which the Benjamites would be allowed to "capture" their daughters as wives. As the girls came out to dance in the festival at Shiloh, the men of Benjamin would be allowed to run out of hiding and grab them and take them home. So, "giving" their daughters would be wrong since they promised not to do that but allowing others to "capture" their daughters would be right, in their eyes, since they did not specifically say that they would not do that. That is the exact sort of mental gymnastics a person does when they leave the firm paths of right and wrong prescribed by God and venture into the uncertain territory of moral relativism. How much better it would have been from start to finish if everyone had obeyed God and done right and none of this from chapters nineteen through twenty-one had ever even taken place!

DO determine that the deciding factor of every decision to be made in your life will be the words, "What does God expect from me? What has He written in His Word on the subject?" If you live your life that way, you will never have to find yourself doing a "dance with deception" such as the children of Israel found themselves doing.

Personal Notes:

_____

_____

_____

_____

_____

_____

_____

_____

_____

_____

_____

_____

_____

_____

Other Books by Dr. Bo Wagner

Beyond the Colored Coat
Daniel: Breathtaking
Don't Muzzle the Ox
Esther: Five Feast and the Finger Prints of God
From Footers to Finish Nails
I'm Saved! Now What???
James: The Pen and the Plumb Line
Marriage Makers/Marriage Breakers
Nehemiah: A Labor of Love
Romans: Salvation From A-Z
Ruth: Diamonds in the Darkness

Fiction Titles

The Night Heroes Series:
Cry From the Coal Mine (Vol. 1)
Free Fall (Vol. 2)
Broken Brotherhood (Vol. 3)
The Blade of Black Crow (Vol. 4)
Ghost Ship (Vol. 5)
When Serpents Rise (Vol. 6)
Moth Man (Vol. 7)
Runaway (Vol. 8)

Sci-Fi

Zak Blue and the Great Space Chase:
Falcon Wing (Vol. 1)